A Time from the World

Rowena Farre

Illustrated by
Alice Pattullo

LITTLE TOLLER BOOKS

This paperback edition published in 2013 by
Little Toller Books
Lower Dairy, Toller Fratrum, Dorset
First published in 1962 by Hutchinson & Co

ISBN 978-1-908213-20-4

Text © The Estate of Rowena Farre 2013
Introduction © Jay Griffiths 2013
Illustrations © Alice Pattullo 2013

We have made every effort to trace the Estate of Rowena Farre;
please notify Little Toller Books with
further information as regards the copyright-holders

Typeset in Monotype Sabon by Little Toller Books
Printed in Spain by GraphyCems, Navarra

All papers used by Little Toller Books
are natural, recyclable products made from
wood grown in sustainable, well-managed forests

A CIP catalogue record for this book is available
from the British Library

3 5 7 9 8 6 4 2 1

CONTENTS

INTRODUCTION   7
Jay Griffiths

1   Tinkers   13

2   On the Move   23

3   Ma   36

4   The Hermit   47

5   Solitary Wandering   60

6   Travelling in Company   70

7   A Pitch Near the Avon   80

8   In the Fields and Elsewhere   93

9   An Invitation   108

10 Home is Where the Heart is   119

11 A Rommerrin   134

12 A Double Life   147

13 Picking   157

14 Hop Harvest   163

15 The Woodyard   177

16 Find a Way or Make One   185

    Glossary   191

INTRODUCTION

Jay Griffiths

'The journey is the thing.'
HOMER, *The Odyssey*

RUNNING AWAY to join the Gypsies can still ring a peal of bells in the human psyche, chiming with the appeal of folk tales to go on the quest, following one's idiosyncratic path through life.

'I had set out on a quest that was to lead me into many byways and highways, a quest not without importance, though the goal was intangible,' writes Rowena Farre, following that calling. As she does, she personifies many of the qualities required of the quester, the folk-tale hero or heroine. She is canny, courageous and kind: she is ingenious. She pays attention to each encounter, translating it for the reader for whom the characters, conversations and situations spring to life. She matches her own opportunism to that of the Gypsies she meets; in the spontaneity of decisions and the craft of the road, she can be as wily as Ulysses on her odyssey.

Born in 1921, she is thought to have spent her early childhood in India, before being sent away to be educated in Britain by her aunt. As a young woman, she trained as a typist and took a variety of office jobs which left her desperate for the open road, and *A Time From the World* describes the Gypsy-journeys Farre took while she was supposed to be at art college.

'You are here to draw what you see,' an art tutor once told her, and this is exactly what she did: *A Time From the World* is written with pen-portraits, sharp delineations of the Gypsies, didikais (half-Gypsies), the tinkers (mainly travelling in Scotland and poorer than Gypsies), as well as the tramps and mumpers ('They call themselves travellers, but the Romanies call them trash,' Farre writes. Mumpers were also known as country tramps who would over-winter, not in towns but in rural areas.)

Gypsy mores, trade, language glint through the book, as well as the dogs, horses, chavvies (children) and the vardo, the Gypsy wagon or caravan. The Gypsy life is not for weaklings, say the Gypsies themselves, and Farre describes the bone-aching harshness of the picking season, when they were employed to harvest peas, beans, strawberries, raspberries, plums, tomatoes, apples, pears and hops. She worked with them while she lived as a traveller, earning money picking or hawking crêpe-paper flowers. She had also picked up a skill in fortune-telling, which the Gypsies themselves wanted her to do for them. Part of this, writes Farre, involves simply being sensitive to what one can see and hear in the client. Further, though, the seer acts as a mirror to the client, seeing 'potentialities, strengths and weaknesses, the sexual inclinations'. Interestingly, though, she will never accept money for doing this, because she wanted the freedom to choose whether or not to say what she saw in the 'dukkering', fortune-telling.

She notes the strain for travellers of being constantly ordered to 'move on' by police and authorities until many Gypsies had given up and were living 'settled' in small houses, and in this the book carries a historic weight, as one of the last close-up portraits of a whole culture at the end of its journey, ordered by the intolerance of modernity to move on, get along: into the past.

It is also, inevitably, a self-portrait – Farre is a complex, paradoxical woman whose pragmatism is interwoven with profound intuition. Half-flint, half-tenderness, she possesses vulnerability: describing her own journey of fear (walking in the woods alone by night) or anger (finding her cherished Victorian snow globe had been filched by chavvies) or the grief at the heart of the book. A shrewd reader of economic motives and manipulating manners, she is attentive to the inner eye and inner ear and to the deep currents of human nature in rebellion against any kind of prison.

'The bedsitter and the Gypsy wagon became symbolic to me. The one represented prison, the other freedom,' she writes, and you can almost hear her gasping for the air of the outdoors life rather than the stifling claustrophobia of the office jobs she must occasionally take.

'How does one emancipate oneself? The question was never out of my mind for long. I heard people in London speak of freedom often enough, but the Gypsies I lived with were people who never mentioned the word freedom,' she writes.

What begins psychologically makes its presence felt stylistically, and as her feet are ravenous for the road, so the rhythm of her writing is a surging, swinging striding: a robust walking style, seldom sedentary apart from the thoughtful asides and broader background views which one imagines written around a camp fire in the evening. It is a fervent, appetitive book, hungry with curiosity, thirsty for vitality.

The story has the pattern of a reel: for a time Farre may catch the hand of a hermit, a child, a lover or a beautiful young man having his hair tonged and oiled, or a grumpy old mumper who created a 'foetid atmosphere caused by the old woman's unwashed person and clothing'. After a time, though, a moment or a month, the fiddle takes up the start of the tune again, and the reel moves her on, as the path moves on through her telling.

Childbirth is here, and abandonment; serenity and squalor; humour and quarrels and the daily difficulties, washing under a tap by a cattle trough, or sitting in the stifling heat of a crowded wagon with the stove burning. She describes a Gypsy rommerin, or wedding: a popular way of meeting, gossiping, getting together and flirting. She writes of the occasional secret Gypsy burial in the woodlands, which would happen when there was no birth certificate for the deceased. The kernel of the book is her own love affair with a man – and she finds herself at the hardest kind of junction where the crossroad is right inside her. It represents a wrenching apart of two paths, a divergence of signposts in the opposition of two significances. Which path she chooses I will not tell you. . .

For all that it is a book in praise of freedom, it is also about Farre's own profound cultural ambivalence and is more than anything an enactment of her own position; for she is a writer and reader in a (mainly) illiterate culture. The situation she finds herself in puts a gulf between those who want the world larger as a result of letters and literature and those who do not or cannot read the world as she does, metaphorically and literally.

Her credo 'to travel my own road' is a fraught phrase because her own road means not only a physical road but also an intellectual one, a literary and metaphoric route she could only take knowing that if she did, it would lead her into 'a world that would often seem dark and unbearably lonely'.

She has, though, a companion on her way, a heroine for me as for Farre: Isabelle Eberhardt. Farre opens the book with a quote from Eberhardt: 'To take the decision, to cast off every bond. . .' Half-Russian, half-French, Eberhardt travelled to north Africa at the end of the nineteenth century, dressed as a young Arab man, and died in a flash flood in the Sahara aged only twenty-seven. A brilliant writer, she was also depressive, alcoholic and passionate with a defiant desire 'to be free and without ties, a nomad camped in life's great desert.'

Rowena Farre honours an ancient nomadism and in the closing paragraph of *A Time From the World*, she draws movingly towards the widest acknowledgement of the Gypsy role: 'The Gypsy lives out for all of us, whatever our nationality or occupation, that which we truly are, travellers of vast and windswept regions whose myriad journeyings will only cease with the ending of time.'

Jay Griffiths
Llanidloes, 2013

To take the decision, to cast off every bond with which modern life and the weakness of our own hearts have chained us, to arm ourselves with the symbolic sack and staff of the pilgrim and *to depart*. . .

ISABELLE EBERHARDT

ONE

Tinkers

THE WAVE SWEPT over the stretch of white beach. In the distance the Island of Lewis floated on the blue-green waters like Tír na nÓg, the Kingdom of Faery. Few people roamed these parts except the crofters who lived here and the wandering tinkers. The white beach stretched away for mile upon mile, both north and south, and you could have it all to yourself. I turned and gazed inland.

I stood on a belt of vivid green machair, or sea grass, which was dotted with pinks and over which strutted several white gulls. Just a short way beyond the machair where the lighter green meadowlands started, was a lonely little croft. This was inhabited by an old tinker couple who, after a lifetime spent travelling, had at last 'settled down'. At least they stayed put during winter and spring. In summer they would lock the door of the croft, give the two goats and the cat into the care of neighbours, and set out once again for the open road. Further inland were five other crofts which comprised the clachan. These were huddled together as though for company. Rounded hills lay in the background. The farther inland the fewer the trees; acres of Ross-and-Cromarty and Sutherland have not got so much as a solitary birch between them.

As I gazed at the scene before me I thought once again how marvellous is the colouring of the landscape in these parts on a fine day. There is a pristine quality about it, and a subtle aura of mystery is imbued in the atmosphere which can be felt but not described.

I sat down on the machair and watched the old woman come out of the byre followed by the two white goats. Every morning the old tinker woman would lead the goats over to a pine strip which lay a short distance from the croft. She would tether them near a stream and in the late afternoon bring them back to the croft for milking.

I had first met this old couple when I was living in Sutherland. They had been travelling the roads in an open cart and sleeping at nights in their tent or in barns. During the day they worked in the fields as pickers. I had got into conversation with them, and they told me that they owned a small croft in Wester Ross and that I would be welcome to put up there with them for a few nights should I ever be in those parts. I had taken them at their word, and for the past two nights I had slept in my sleeping bag on the floor of the croft parlour. The old man and woman slept on a large mattress on the floor of the one small bedroom.

My plan for the approaching summer months was to travel with tinkers for a while, then wend my way further south into England and spend the rest of the summer and autumn with Gypsy friends. I knew many Gypsies, but my acquaintanceship with tinkers was limited to this one couple, for though I had spoken to many families of tinkers I had met on the roads and in the Fort William district I had yet to travel with them. I had hoped that my elderly friends, whose names were Mr Connor Digby and Mrs Maggie Digby, would be able to put me in touch with other members of their fraternity. But all their relatives and friends roamed these far northern areas, and they said they knew few tinkers who travelled further south, the direction in which I was heading. So it seemed that after all I would have to make my own contacts with these people.

The old woman walked slowly towards the pine strip, the two goats following dutifully at her heels. Rain or shine, she always wore a shawl over her head which she removed only in the croft. She had told me that she was in her mid-seventies. But this I rather doubted in spite of her deeply wrinkled skin, tanned a deep russet through living for decades in the open air. It is the habit of both tinker and Gypsy women to add several years to their age once the middle years are past, for the elderly matriarch has an honourable place amongst these people. I mentally deducted ten years from Mrs Digby's stated age. Of course she had no knowledge of the precise year or month in which she was born – few of the older Gypsies and tinkers have, for children's birthdays are never celebrated, nor are their babies usually officially registered at an office.

I walked over to the croft. Mr Connor Digby was sitting on a cane chair outside the building smoking his pipe. He performed the minimum of chores in the smallholding which adjoined the croft, and it was a mystery to their neighbours how the pair got the necessary cash to live even the simple existence they did.

'It was very kind of you and your wife to put me up,' I said. 'I've enjoyed my stay with you both immensely. I'll be leaving tomorrow and going down to Fort William.'

'Ach, dinna go tomorrow,' the old man said at once.

'I must start moving south before long,' I said.

'There's plenty o' time yet before the picking season starts, and there's a wee job I'd like ye to do for me afore ye leave.'

'What is it?' I asked.

'D'ye ken anything about money?'

'Money?' I said with surprise.

'Aye.'

'Well, a little,' I answered dubiously.

It is one of the misfortunes of my life that my monetary knowledge is extremely limited; money had come my way in the smallest of dribs and drabs. 'Anyway,' said Mr Digby with assurance, 'ye've had more experience wi' money than I have.'

'Oh, I certainly wouldn't say that!'

'I reckon ye have, and ye know all about postal savings books and banks?'

'Well. . .'

'I thought so. Come inside a moment,' he said, raising a finger to indicate strict secrecy.

We sat down at the table.

'Now I'll tell ye about the wee job I want ye to do for me. And you must gie me your word that ye won't say naught to them about it.'

The 'them', I gathered, meant his crofter neighbours.

'Aye, them's a rare sneaking, inquisitive lot. But I reckon you can trust the chaps who work in the banks.'

He walked over to a cupboard and opened a drawer. 'When we go awa' in the summer we leave this sack under a floorboard and trust to luck that they won't unlock the door and sneak about in here and discover it. But we're taking a risk, ye must admit.'

'You certainly are,' I said, not having the vaguest idea what he was talking about, though I gathered that money was involved somewhere.

He undid the string and opened out the neck of a medium-sized flour sack which had once contained something like four pounds of flour but which now contained pounds of a different order.

He tipped up the sack, and coins and notes rose in a mound on the table. I gasped.

'How much about d'ye reckon there was in the sack?'

'About two hundred pounds?' I ventured.

'Well, I tell ye there's more than five hundred. We've been saving up for the past fifteen years. What I want ye to do is to go along to the township tomorrow and have it put in the bank for us. Will ye do that?'

'Yes, if you wish it,' I said without enthusiasm.

'I've already opened a small account there. I think it would be best if ye put this in for us as ye've had more experience handling money.'

I was about to protest, but he held up a hand. 'I'm not much guid at dealing wi' large sums at banks, and I reckon they'd find it easier if ye did the job for me.'

He handed me a scrap of paper on which he had written in rounded handwriting that I, Miss Rowena Farre, had been delegated by himself, Mr Connor Digby, to pay in the money – uncounted – contained in the sack, to his current account.

I was somewhat surprised that he was able to write, for few tinkers of his age can do so, having had next to no schooling. As I was putting the slip of paper away in a pocket, Mrs Digby came through the door.

'Aye, Maggie, she'll go along for us.'

'That's fine,' Mrs Digby said, then turning to me – 'And you can do a bit o' shopping for yourself while you're there and maybe get a few odds and ends for me too. Take the early bus and come back by the late one. That'll give ye a guid day in the township.'

Somewhat overwhelmed by the task which had been allotted me, I sat down by the peat fire and accepted a strong cup of tea.

My hostess removed the scarf from her head and sat down opposite me. She wore her white hair plaited and coiled over her ears, Gypsy fashion.

'When I was a younger woman it was a dark red,' she said, when I complimented her on its whiteness. It had not got that yellow tinge old people's hair often has.

'Connor always says it was my red hair that first attracted him when I was working in the fields wi' my family. I was around fifteen or sixteen at the time and we were married that same season. I don't mean, o' course, that we were wedded in a kirk. We were only officially wedded last year by the minister, as I've told ye.'

It seemed that the minister had persuaded them to get married in the kirk and had instructed them in the wedding service. Now they were officially wed and were proud of the fact. Moreover, the minister had presented them with a copy of the Bible and every evening, before

going to 'bed' on the mattress, Mr Digby would read out a portion
from the Book.

We were not let off that evening, and no sooner had we finished
our supper of fried tomatoes, sausages and bread, swilled down with
several cups of tea, than Mr Digby took the Bible from a shelf and began
thumbing slowly through the pages. I groaned inwardly. Time meant
nothing to the old man and on the first evening of my stay the reading
had seemed to go on for well over an hour. Presently he stopped turning
over the leaves and said to me, 'Well maybe this evening you'd like to
choose a chapter for me to read out. Is there any special piece you'd
like?'

'I should like you to read the story of Joseph and the coat of many
colours,' I said, 'and how the brothers threw him into a well and he was
sold into Egypt.'

I found the chapter in Genesis, Mr Digby raised a patriarchal hand,
and the reading started.

'Now Israel loved Joseph more than all his children because he were
the son o' his auld age, and he made him a coat o' many colours. And
when his brethren saw that their father loved him more than all his
brethren, they hated him and could nae speak peaceably unto him. . .'

The paraffin lamp cast a warm light over the old tinker as he sat at
the table, one finger following the line of print. The goats munched their
fodder in the byre next door and every so often stamped a hoof, the cat
lay curled up in front of the fire, and Mrs Digby sat listening attentively,
her hands clasped together on her lap. Occasionally my thoughts strayed
to the pinewoods outside, to the waves rushing up the beach, then back
to the sonorous voice: 'And Joseph was the governor over the land, and
he it was that sold to all the people o' the land. And Joseph's brethren
came, and bowed down themselves before him wi' their faces to the
earth. . .'

Finally, Mr Digby closed the Bible. The reading had come to an end.

The next morning the old tinker woman cooked me a good breakfast
and the sack was taken from the drawer once more and put into a large

wicker basket of the type which is used for hawking. Then it was covered over with a checked cloth.

'You shouldn't find it too heavy,' said Mr Digby.

'They are going to have quite a job counting the money up at the bank,' I said.

'Aye, just tell them to take their time. And don't take the track past the crofts – keep clear o' that lot o' busybodies. Take the track which leads through the birch spinney. And don't get talking wi' anyone on the way to the bus stop.'

'Very well,' I said, already in a state of nerves at the thought of having to transport safely to the township such a large sum of money.

'If ye *should* meet up wie one o' them sneakin' crofters and he asks ye what ye have in the basket, just tell him it's a few pounds o' new potatoes you're taking to the township to sell at the grocer's.'

'Very well,' I replied.

The basket, as I discovered soon enough, was terribly heavy. I hurried along with a beating heart and aching arms, occasionally casting a suspicious glance towards the crofts.

It was as I was walking through the birch spinney that I heard, to my horror, a voice call 'Guid morning!' just behind me. I said nothing but hurried on faster.

'Hie! Canna ye wait a wee while?'

Then I heard the sound of running footsteps and a young man appeared at my side.

'I called out 'Guid morning' to ye. Dinna ye hear?'

'Good morning,' I said.

'Are ye catching the bus to the township?'

'Yes, I am.'

'So am I. I'll take that basket from ye. It looks heavy from the way you are walking along.'

'Oh, it's not heavy!' And I clutched the handle with all my strength.

I had taken a surreptitious glance at the young man. He appeared honest enough – but appearances are often deceptive. I could not afford to take any chances with the load I was carrying.

'Here, gie that to me,' he insisted. 'I'll carry it for ye.' And he seized hold of the handle and dragged the basket from me. 'Please give it back!' I said desperately, making a final attempt to regain it. 'Come on. We must hurry or we'll miss the bus. My, you've certainly got a load under that cloth – what is it?'

'Potatoes,' I said firmly.

'Potatoes!' He looked at me as though I were overdue for a session with a psychiatrist.

'New potatoes. . .'

'Potatoes wouldn't be that heavy.'

He dug a finger at the checked cloth under which lay the precious sack. It feels more like doubloons – certainly not potatoes,' he said with a laugh.

I shuddered at the nearness of his guess.

'Look,' I said desperately, 'I've undertaken a job for the old tinker couple and they don't want me to let out what it is.'

'I see. But they've no right to gie ye a load this weight. Where will you be taking it to when you reach the township? I'll gie you a hand there.'

'To the bank,' I replied thoughtlessly.

'To the bank. Then it is money.'

'Please!'

'How much is under the cloth – d'ye ken?'

'I haven't the faintest idea,' I replied, 'except that it's a goodly sum.'

'I'll say it is. Don't worry; I won't say anything to the other crofters about it. We've all been wondering these past few days why it is you're staying wi' an old tinker couple like them. Tinkers are not the sort o' people you can trust. One thing about that old pair, they keep more or less to themselves. We don't want too many o' that sort about the place.'

We reached the stop about half a minute before the bus. In spite of my previous anxiety about the young crofter accompanying me, I now felt rather glad of his presence. It would be a relief to have someone go with me to the bank and get the money passed safely over the counter.

On alighting from the bus, we made straight for the bank. I handed the slip of paper Mr Digby had given me to a clerk.

My new-found companion left in order to attend to some affairs of his own, and I sat down while the counting commenced. The clerk untied the bag and extracted a handful of notes and coins, giving me a none too friendly look as he did so.

An hour passed and he was still counting. The looks he now flung at me were positively murderous. Whenever a dearth of other customers permitted, another clerk joined him and they carried on the counting together. Notes and heaps of coins were piled up on the counter but still the sack was not empty.

'Can I come back after lunch?' I asked tentatively.

'You sit there till we've finished counting,' the clerk snapped, 'then you sign a receipt.'

I sat.

Some two hours later the sackful of notes and coins had been totted up, and I signed a receipt for the sum of five hundred and ninety-three pounds, sixteen shillings and threepence halfpenny which was to be entered to the old tinker's account.

'And don't come in here again with another sack full of money,' said the clerk.

'I can assure you I won't,' I said.

I walked outside with a sigh of thankfulness that my task had been finally completed.

After a light snack, I did some shopping, took a quick look round the township, then met my companion for high tea.

As I buttered a slice of toast and started off on a plate of haddock cooked in milk, he asked, 'How much cash was there?'

I told him.

'Whew!' he exclaimed. 'Fancy that old tinker couple saving up a big sum like that.'

It was quite late when we got back – somewhere around nine o'clock. Even so, I was somewhat surprised when I arrived at the croft to find it in darkness and the old couple already gone to bed. I called out to them, but not a sound came from the bedroom except an occasional snore. They had no doubt reckoned that my temper would not be at its best on my return from the township, and that it might be as well if we did not meet again till the following morning after a night's sleep had restored me to a more equable frame of mind. And in this they were right.

Over a breakfast of porridge, bacon and eggs, they thanked me warmly for having done the job.

'There is one thing I think I ought to tell you, Mr Digby,' I said, and I related how the young crofter had carried the basket to the bank and knew that the sack had contained a large sum of money.

The old couple appeared startled for a moment.

'And when the money was counted, did ye tell him how much there was?' Mr Digby asked.

'Yes, I did,' I confessed. 'He was naturally curious and asked me how much the sack had contained.'

'Well,' he said after a pause, 'as the money's in the bank now I don't suppose it matters.'

He gave a slow smile, and I had the feeling that he was secretly pleased that the crofters would know that an old tinker couple like themselves had managed to save through the years such a large sum of money.

Soon after breakfast, I fastened the straps of my rucksack and, waving goodbye to them, set off for Fort William.

TWO

On the Move

THE AREA round about Fort William is much frequented by tinkers and it did not take me long to find out that a group of them was encamped a few miles from the town. But it is one thing to know where tinkers are camped and another to get yourself on sufficiently good terms with them so that they welcome you among them as a fellow traveller.

I bought a supply of food in the town, then walked back on my tracks to where I had been told their bothies were pitched. In the north the tents are called bothies and in the south tans.

I came to a lane down which was bicycling a farm worker and I asked him the whereabouts of the tinkers. He pointed towards a clump of hawthorns in the distance.

'Behind them trees, that's where they're pitched. It's about a ten-minute walk from the farmhouse.'

I walked slowly towards the spot the man had indicated. Soon I came to a narrow stream, the banks of which were dotted with furze bushes. Across the water I could see that the tinkers had pitched two bothies by the side of their carts, and their horses were grazing untethered in the field. There were two women and some children on the campsite. They soon caught sight of me and stood motionless, watching me approach. I did not go up to them direct. I pretended to be quite oblivious of their presence and started to erect my small nylon tent a short way from the stream, in the lee of some furze bushes. The tent erected, I filled my kettle from the stream and started to prepare high tea.

It was not long before two children – a boy and a girl – came wandering over. Their faces showed that look peculiar to the travelling folk when meeting up with a stranger, which expresses neither friendliness nor hostility but a quietly watchful state. Having stood staring at me for some seconds, the boy said bluntly, 'What are ye doing here?'

'Cooking high tea,' I replied.

'Aye. But why've ye come and pitched right near us?'

'Near you?' I said. 'I'm nowhere near you. You're right the other side of the stream. I think this is a very pleasant place to set up my tent, that's all.'

'Are ye going to work on the farm?' asked the girl.

'Maybe.'

'D'ye always cook on that wee stove?' she questioned again.

'Not always. Sometimes I cook on an open fire, like you folks. But I'm not going to the bother of lighting one this evening.'

'So ye're going to sleep tonight in that wee tent?' said the boy.

'Yes, I am.'

'I reckon it won't keep the rain out if it starts coming down.'

'That's just where you're wrong,' I said, 'because it does.'

I opened a bag of sweets and put one into my mouth. They both asked for one and I gave them a single sweet apiece. As they now considered the ice broken between us, they set to inspecting my belongings. I did not take my eyes off them a moment for I knew full well that if I did several bits of my belongings might find their way across the stream. Pilfering is not uncommon among some groups of tinkers.

'What are your names?' I asked.

'She's Janie and I'm Brian.'

'And what's your family name?'

'Taff.'

I pointed to the bothies. 'Are you all one family over there?'

'Nay. There's me and Janie, Ma and Dad. And we travel wi' our cousins. They're called Mackintosh and they've a boy called Leslie and a wee bairn.'

'How old is Leslie?'

'Round about eight.'

A woman appeared on the scene. 'You pitching here?' she asked.

'For a couple of nights.'

'That's our Ma,' said the girl.

This woman was reserved and far from friendly, and I guessed she strongly resented my presence. Her dark red hair fell to her shoulders, and she was dressed in a cotton blouse and an old flowered cotton skirt. I noted that two of her fingers were bandaged with strips of dirty linen. Curiosity is something tinkers understand for they are not lacking in a good streak of it themselves, though they nevertheless are often resentful of it in others. I pointed to her hand and asked, 'Have you cut your fingers?'

'I cut them opening a tin,' she replied.

'Then I hope you put some iodine on the cuts; tins can be very poisonous,' I said in the manner of one who has passed a course in nursing. 'What sort of tin was it?' I asked, stirring a mess of baked beans in my pan.

She appeared a little uneasy. 'It was just a tin o' baked beans like those you're warming up, only they were in tomato sauce.'

'Um. . . Still, there's nothing to worry about if you did dab the cuts with iodine.'

'Is that medicines in that case over there?' she asked, indicating my first-aid case which had been dropped on the grass by the children with various other pieces of my belongings.

'Yes – medicine, bandages, scissors and so on,' I replied.

'Perhaps ye could let me have a bandage,' she said. 'This one could do wi' a change.'

'Certainly.'

She stripped off the dirty bandages, washed the cuts in the stream, then I applied a little iodine and put clean bandages on her fingers. She and the children appeared to enjoy this little first-aid session.

By the time the two men returned from the farm I was on good terms with both the women and the children.

The following morning, at the invitation of the men, I moved my tent and belongings over to their side of the field. Now I was welcome to their fire as well as their company. The two men set off to the farm after an early breakfast while the women did chores about the camp. Then I and the younger woman, Brenda Mackintosh, walked to the farmhouse to enquire whether the farmer's wife could give us any jobs for the day. This was the period of odd jobs before the picking season got under way.

The only job the farmer's wife could give us was plucking fowls; peculiarly distasteful work, so far as I am concerned. The two of us sat on wooden chairs under which had been spread newspapers, and we plucked and plucked bunches of feathers from the birds. They were going to be taken into Fort William next day for sale. At the end of the morning the farmer's wife gave us each ten shillings and told us that there would be no further work until the morrow.

This tinker woman, Brenda, was not so good looking as the other. She was heavily built with a round plump face and black permed hair. But now that we had become acquainted I found her less aloof than the other.

'Where will ye be going when ye leave here?' she asked me as we walked back to camp over the short turf, out of which sprang the curled fronds of young bracken.

'I shall be making for England, the west of England,' I said.

'I'll be spending summer and autumn there picking, maybe the winter.'

'Will ye be travelling alone?'

'No, with Romany friends,' and I added: 'I've just come from Wester Ross where I've been staying with an old tinker couple called Connor and Maggie Digby. Have you heard of them?'

She shook her head.

'They only travel in summer now,' I said. 'Before I cross the border, I should like to spend a short spell travelling with tinkers. Just a couple of days maybe. Do you think I might come along with you for a while when you leave here? I'm willing to go hawking and pay my own way, of course.'

'I don't know,' she said, 'but I'll ask the men if you like.'

'Thank you.'

And there I left the matter. I had no intention of bringing it up again. If they were agreeable to my proposition they would soon let me know, otherwise they would not mention it and we would part as though I had not spoken of my wish to travel with them.

Brenda's husband, Spencer, was a tall burly man, slow of speech but very quick with his hands. As we sat round the fire after tea that day he joined in the conversation only occasionally but busied himself carving pegs with his penknife from lengths of stripped alder. Having dexterously carved one, he would toss it into a wooden box by his side. Neither of the two couples, as I soon found out, had been officially married. Like most of their kind, they apparently looked on official ceremonies with indifference.

All the members of this group, with the exception of Ellen Taff, the red-haired woman, had been born in bothies and had never known anything but the travellers' life. Ellen's early life, so her husband Forsyth told me, had been a little different from theirs. He had first met her when he was picking in the Morven district. Her parents were both tinkers but had 'settled', and it seemed that Ellen was destined to lead a householder's existence. In fact, she had already accepted the proposal of a farmer's boy to become his wife. Then Forsyth appeared on the scene, much to her parents' dismay, and proposed to her after only a few days' acquaintances. She had accepted him, and without a word to the parents, who had done their best to keep him away from their daughter, they had slipped off and got wedded according to tinker custom, out in the open fields, with an old tinker performing the tying of hands ceremony. I was to witness this ceremony for myself later that year when a Gypsy girl I knew called Thurzie was married to a young Romany.

'And have you ever wished to go back to the settled life?' I asked Ellen.

'Nay, never,' she replied. These were the first words she had spoken, so far as I could recollect, during the whole evening. She continued in a low voice, 'I reckon that I had always wanted to lead the travelling life because I guessed it would be the only life to make me happy.' And she gave one of her rare but beautiful smiles.

I had occasionally seen this smile before in Scotland. It expresses, in the slow movement of the lips, the qualities of gentleness, pride, a depth of experience, and a certain mystery. There is nothing shallow or superficial about it; it is not the smile of a flirt or coquette. I have seen this smile again on women's faces in India, and on the upturned lips of ancient Athenian statues. Perhaps the women of Greece still smile in this way.

I said goodnight and walked over to my tent. I undressed, sponged my face and hands with a flannel, and got into my sleeping bag. By the light of a torch, balanced on top of the rucksack, I started to read a book of Hans Andersen's Fairy Tales. A slight noise just outside the tent made me glance towards the opening and I saw that two hands were holding the flap apart and two pairs of eyes were looking in at me.

'It's just us,' came Janie's voice, on seeing that she and her brother had been spotted.

'What do you want?' I asked. The flap was drawn more widely apart. 'We just want to hae another look at that crystal ball o' yours, Reena,' said the boy, using the name I am called among travellers.

They had clearly been delving into my rucksack when I was absent, for I kept this ball right at the bottom and had not taken it out since my arrival.

'When did you first see this ball?' I asked.

'This morning,' Brian replied, 'when ye were over at the farm.'

The pair had now been joined by their cousin Leslie and the three sat crouched outside in the dusk watching me intently.

'You mean,' I said severely, 'that you've been looking over my belongings while I was out. Would you please not do that again. You've no right to.'

'Aye,' they murmured.

'Can we come in now,' Janie asked, 'and hae a look at it?'

'Very well,' I said.

Removing the torch from the rucksack, I looked inside. My belongings were in a state of topsy-turvy.

'I'll be mad if you go looking through my things again,' I said, extracting the ball.

They said nothing but sat on their haunches, waiting expectantly. The small tent was full to overflowing and it was hardly possible to move an elbow.

I held the ball in my hand. It was a Victorian children's toy, about the size of a small orange in which a little scene had been set. This scene was of a village along whose streets walked a man and woman, arm-in-arm, dressed in the clothes of the period; in front of them walked a tiny dog. An old man, bent over a stick, was coming towards the couple. The village was surrounded by rugged mountains dotted with pine trees. It might have been a scene from any district hereabouts. When the ball was shaken a snowstorm whirled, and for a while everything would be blotted out until the snow slowly came to rest again on mountains, roofs and streets. I had possessed this pretty toy for many years, and I would often shake it and watch the descending snow. If I should be working in a town the glass ball had the gift of transporting me to the countryside. To call it a toy seemed hardly the right word, for it had often proved itself to be something of a magic crystal, setting my imagination free from whatever surroundings I happened to be in. And I had often noted that it had a fascination for others, grown-ups and children alike, besides myself.

I handed them the ball and the three of them played with it happily for about an hour while I continued to read my book. They made up stories about the little people and dog, and gazed into its depths like fortune-tellers trying to glimpse the future.

'I'm going to sleep now,' I said.

They handed back the ball, then, crawling from the tent, ran over to the bothies.

The next morning the two men decided to move on that day and started to pull up the curved stakes over which the canvas had been flung. Presently Forsyth came over to me.

'We're moving today,' he said. 'If ye'd like to travel wie us for a while you're welcome.'

'Thanks,' I said, and started to dismantle my own tent and pack away my belongings.

The two horses were caught and harnessed to the shafts of the carts. Everything was then piled in. Travelling with tinkers in an open cart can be hard when the weather is bad. But on the morning we set off, although the sky was grey and the breeze somewhat chilly, there was a pleasant freshness and clarity in the atmosphere and the countryside could be seen for miles around. The carts rattled off down the lane. The men did the driving while the women and children were split up between the two carts. It was only after we had been going down a lonely country road for what must have been a good half-hour that I suddenly thought to ask where we were heading.

'You're all right,' Forsyth said over his shoulder. 'We're heading south towards Glencoe way. We'll be camping out in the open tonight.'

By which he meant, I gathered, that we would not be camping in the vicinity of a farm or clachan.

The carts were rattling down roads well off the main highways. The horses' hooves flicked up stones from the unsurfaced road. Over to our left rose Ben Nevis and the wild mountain country. At midday we made a brief halt. A roadside fire was lit, the kettle brought to the boil for cups of tea. But no cooking was done. We ate bread, cheese, and slices of cake.

That afternoon we came to a small clachan where a jumble sale was being held in the hall. On seeing the people going in, the tinker women decided at once to go in too, and look over the goods for sale. They hurried across with the children. I stayed with the men by the carts. We had hardly halted there a minute when a policeman came pedalling up on a bicycle and, seeing the tinkers, got off and asked, 'Will you be moving on soon?'

'In a short while,' Spencer replied.

'Are you trading round here?'

'Nay. The women have just gone inside there to see if they can get some clothes cheap.'

'Where are you making for?'

'Glencoe way.'

'I see.' He mounted his bicycle and rode off.

It is extraordinary what the traveller today has to put up with from officialdom, the personal questioning and so on, should he halt his cart for only a brief while. Yet I do not forget – and neither do the travellers – that in Britain, although officialdom is doing everything it possibly can to make travellers 'settle' and generally make their lives difficult, our native nomads have not been persecuted, murdered, or forced into factories, which they consider as prisons, which has been the case in many other European countries. The traveller in Britain has a greater degree of freedom than in many other parts of the world, and in spite of much grumbling, he is at heart grateful that he was born here and not, for example, in Germany.

The women and children came out of the hall, their arms and baskets filled with a conglomeration of old clothing and shoes.

'We'll try on some o' these later,' said Brenda, holding up a cardigan to see whether there were any moth-holes which had escaped her eye in the hall. 'Anything that turns out nae guid we'll chop later.'

The word 'chop' is used both by tinkers and Gypsies and means to exchange or barter something for other goods.

Amongst the bargains they had just acquired was a large straw hat, almost Edwardian in its size, round which was a large blue velvet bow pinned to which was a squashed yellow rose. Ellen put the hat on her head.

'Whatever did ye want to go and buy that for?' asked Forsyth in the tone of voice used by many a husband whose wife has just purchased some outrageous piece of headgear.

'I liked it,' she replied. 'We can always chop it later.'

'We! Ye'll chop it yerself. I wouldn't be seen dead wi' a thing like that.'

But strangely enough, Ellen with her untidy dark red hair, looked beautiful wearing that battered straw hat. Old fashioned though it was and fit only for the dustbin, it nevertheless suited her and with her woman's instinct she had sensed this. Unfortunately, there would be few opportunities when she could wear it and it would doubtless change hands again in a few days' time.

The horses clip-clopped at a slow pace down the road. The grey dusk of evening shortened the view. A flock of starlings flew by.

'This place will do,' Spencer called from the leading cart, reining in the horse.

The carts were parked on a wide grass verge which bordered a pinewood. The animals were taken from the shafts and firmly tethered. Then the bothies and my tent were set up under the pine branches. A fire was lit on a sandy patch of ground and the iron crane set over it, a cooking pot suspended from the hooked portion. It was still light enough to see the yellow clumps of primroses growing amongst the undergrowth and a few white heads of anemones or wind-flowers. By a blackthorn tree, whose twigs still showed only a trace of green leaf, was a furze bush on which were blooming several bright yellow flowers which smelt pleasantly of apricots. I thought of hot summer days out on moorlands covered with 'the ever blossoming furze' bushes, when the scent from the flowers had been quite overpowering.

'One of the things I like best about the woods in Britain,' I said, on returning to the fire from which thick, heavy plumes of smoke were ascending skywards, 'is that except under certain trees, there is always plenty of undergrowth, moss, flowers and so on.'

'Well, o' course,' said Forsyth.

'That's far from being the case in many eastern countries,' I said. 'In Morocco there are cork forests stretching for acres and there is hardly a blade of grass under their branches. And you can motor for miles over the countryside – days sometimes – without seeing more vegetation than a few scraggy bushes.'

'Then I never want to go to Morocco when I grow up,' said Leslie, chaining one of the long-legged dogs to the cart.

We had meat and vegetables for supper that evening and, of course, the inevitable cups of tea.

How peaceful it is under the pine branches, I thought, as I sat for a while outside my tent before going to sleep. It was weeks now since I had read a newspaper or listened to the radio. I wanted only to live my own life which, as I realised from my very early years, was set in a totally different direction from the lives of most people in the class in which I had been born. Not that I had any desire to attach myself to any other class; I wished to free myself from all artificial barriers.

It was because of this determination that, in early adulthood, I started to lead a secret life. I began to correspond with foreigners, some of whom I had met for brief periods when they visited Britain, and this correspondence had by now reached large proportions. And I started to travel, first at home, later overseas. Thus began my life with the Gypsies, my secret life which ran parallel with a more conventional life at an art school and in various offices. To me, of course, the secret life was by far the more important, but they remained linked, these two lives, and I never managed to break free of the one and live the other entirely, hard though I tried. I was to experience the dual existence of a slave (for town and office life were like slavery to me) and a free being during those years: to plunge continually from one state to the other. How does one emancipate oneself? The question was never out of my mind for long. I heard people in London speak of freedom often enough, but the Gypsies I lived with were people who never mentioned the word freedom, who perhaps in their whole lives had hardly given it a thought, but who were nevertheless relatively free beings, able to communicate fully and freely with others, unselfconscious and spontaneous in their behaviour.

I never accepted the periods of slavery in office and bedsitter, yet I was not able to lead my other life except in comparatively brief stretches. Circumstances and sometimes my own desires continually hauled me back to a humdrum and narrow existence: money, a taste for the cultural side of town life, my talent for writing, which at one moment I would see as my greatest barrier to freedom and at another as the means of attaining it – financial freedom, at least. All these things would bring me back sooner or later to the office desk or drawing board, until I kicked over the traces and set off once more to lead the free life of a traveller.

The bedsitter and the Gypsy wagon became symbolic to me. The one represented prison, the other freedom. I had set out on a quest that was to lead me into many byways and highways, a quest not without importance, though the goal was intangible. Through living the simple open air life of a nomad I found I was in touch with deeper levels of existence, and so my days passed by more harmoniously and vividly and I saw nature with clearer eyes. I did not guess that evening, encamped under the pine branches, that soon I would be facing a critical turning point in my life and should have to decide whether or not to join the travelling fraternity for good. Nor did I know that my final decision was to bring me to the verge of despair. All that lay hidden in the future. And later, glancing back, I would remember how calm and serene I was that night as I watched through the tent opening the dim outlines of a tufted pine stem being swung in the breeze.

I travelled with these tinkers for five days. I went hawking with the women, a basket filled with pegs and cheap jewellery over my arm. And I shopped with them too in the little country stores of lonely clachans. My accentless voice, and perhaps something about my looks – my skin was untanned then – always made the shopkeepers glance at me in surprise, and an enquiring look would spread across their faces as though they longed to ask me what I was doing in the company of tinkers.

Later, when my complexion had darkened a little, I was often taken to be a Gypsy by the gorgio fraternity just so long as I did not speak. People seeing me going along a village street with a basket over my arm or sitting in a cart with other travellers never took me for anyone but a Romany. But I had only to enter a shop and ask for a packet of tea or enquire of a village woman whether she wanted any pegs, and the fact that I was not a born and bred traveller would be immediately apparent to them, and arouse their curiosity as to why I should have attached myself to a group of tinkers or Gypsies.

One morning, not many miles from Ballachulish, we started to cross a moorland dotted with pine trees and furze bushes in the middle of which was a crossroads. The tinkers were taking a road which led westwards. They were making for a farm where they had been given work in the past. I was taking the road leading south. I climbed down from the cart and my belongings were handed to me.

'Goodbye,' I called as the horses moved off down the straight stretch of road.

'Goodbye,' they called back. 'See ye again one day, maybe.'

I sat down at the crossing and waited for some vehicle to come by and hitch a lift on it. It was quite possible I would have to wait an hour or so as traffic was infrequent over these lonely moors. As I sat there, something made me undo the straps of my rucksack and feel inside for the glass ball. My fingers pried here and there seeking it, but it was no good. I knew that however long I searched my fingers would not touch the glass again.

Perhaps that Victorian glass ball is still with those tinker children, or perhaps having enjoyed it for a little while they chopped it for something else. I do not begrudge it to them. And I like to think of them, pitched at some camping ground, staring at the little scene and watching the snow whirl, as I used to do sometimes in bygone years.

THREE

Ma

I SPENT OVER A WEEK slowly wending my way down through the borderlands and the Lake District. I was in no hurry, for I still had some weeks to fill in before I was due to meet the Boswell family of Gypsies at a stopping place, or hatchin-tan near Evesham. This was the third year I had arranged to spend part of the picking season with them.

Roughly, the nomads of Britain can be divided into the following groups. First come the Gypsies, the aristocrats, as it were, at least they look upon themselves as being so. Although it is now thought that the Gypsies came from India this still has not been proved for certain and doubtless never will be. Romany, their traditional language, contains a good many words which are derivations of Hindi. The Gypsies are a traditional and conservative people with an ancestry stretching back into the distant past. They have been nomads throughout the centuries, with their own customs, superstitions, laws, herbal cures and poisons, and their own unique way of life. The women are independent, proud, strong, yet feminine. Servility has never been one of their characteristics. Both sexes, male and female, are looked upon as having equal but different parts to play in life, neither one superior to the other, and both the men and the women hold considerable power in their different spheres. The women have always been the 'doctors' in the tribes, and still are to this day. The men maintain tribal law and order.

Half-breed Gypsies are called didikais or posh-rats. The Boswells, the Lees, and the Smiths are the largest Gypsy families in Britain.

The tinkers, who only travel in Scotland, have always been natives of these Islands. They have less tradition behind them than the Gypsies and are less wealthy. Many only possess bothies, though quite a few nowadays also own wagons and trailers. Their main trade used to be, of course, mending pots and pans. Now they earn their living chiefly by picking and the selling of scrap-iron and logs, as is the case with the Gypsies. Their women are not so much given to hawking as their nomadic sisters further south, nor, in the land of second sight, do many of them possess it or tell fortunes.

Last come the tramps and mumpers. These are not travellers in the true sense of the word as applied to the Gypsies and tinkers. The difference between a tramp and a mumper is that the former usually spends his winters in one of our big cities, in a doss house, or he may rent a cheap little room in a tenement. The mumper is the country tramp and spends his winters in some shack or an old wagon bought cheap from the Gypsies. Lack of money is not usually the main reason why these people, whether men or women, take to the road. There is usually some psychological problem, or some deep-seated unhappiness in them. Occasionally one meets with a really happy tramp who lives the life simply because he wants to, but he is something of a rarity. Most of them are dirty, unhappy, lonely, often bitter and difficult people. If they get themselves off the road after a year or two they may well settle down to regular work and better lives. If not, the road has got them and they find it almost impossible, even though they may wish it, to break away from a nomadic existence.

With the Gypsies and tinkers I felt a definite sense of kinship. This was something I had not felt so far in the case of the tramp and mumper fraternity, and when the opportunity offered itself of travelling with an old mumper woman, I confess I did not relish the idea. I was warned to leave my gold earrings behind, and Gypsy friends told me I would have to take a good all-over wash and have my clothes disinfected before I joined up with them again. But I wanted to round off my experience of the lives of every sort of traveller – not the best reason, I admit, for keeping company with another person.

It was on a farm in Shropshire, when I was working along a row of peas with a Gypsy couple in whose wagon I was staying, that an old mumper woman who went by the name of Ma, had come up to me and asked for a peppermint in a voice that was a hoarse whisper. She had presumably seen me take a packet of mints from my pocket and put one into my mouth. I had given her one and she had moved off slowly in the manner of a sleepwalker. In the late afternoon of the same day, as I was packing up and rubbing my stained fingers on a handkerchief and trying to straighten out, she had come up to me again and in a soft wheedling voice informed me that she had no milk or potatoes.

'Then why don't you buy some at the farm?' I said.

There followed a long, significant pause.

'Have you no money?'

'No love. I hadn't got none when I came, and the farmer don't like paying off till the last day. I only want a couple o' spuds and a cupper milk.'

How I dislike this servile form of begging!

'Very well,' I told her, 'I'll let you have a few spuds and a cup of milk. Don't follow me now – I'll bring them over to your hut.'

'Thank you, dearie.'

When I went over with an enamel cupful of milk and some potatoes, she and another woman, who had a dissolute, meretricious appearance, were seated in the doorway of a hut peeling several large potatoes.

'I thought you said you had no —' I began.

'They're mine, sweetheart,' said the meretricious creature in a sneering voice. She was wearing a wealth of cheap jewellery and had drawn an uneven line of scarlet lipstick across her thin lips. The Romany women seldom wear any jewellery unless it is real gold.

'I see,' I said.

'Yes, they're hers, duck,' said Ma. 'I'm just lending a hand. Thanks very much for this lot. I'll pour the milk into my mug.' The other woman gave me a sharp glance. 'My name's Saluki Waine. What's yours?'

'Reena.'

'Reena what?'

'Reena Farre.'

'Well, that's a pretty name, I must say.'

Ma had emerged from the hut with an enamel jug filled to the brim with milk.

'That'll keep us going nicely,' she remarked, with a wavering smile.

They had won this round in the mumper's day-to-day task of getting something for nothing, and they wanted me to know it, moreover.

'You travelling with them Gyps?' asked Saluki. 'Yes,' I replied, adding to myself – thank God I'm not travelling with either of you! So what followed was somewhat curious.

Ma sidled up to me and placed one filthy hand on my shoulder. 'Why don't you travel with me a day or two? I'm making for a railway wagon on a small holding. It's a beautiful spot.'

'Where is the wagon?' I asked, out of curiosity.

She pointed vaguely to the east, the direction where more or less all the travellers were heading. 'How many days?' I asked again. 'Just a day and a half's travelling, duck. It's ever such a pretty spot.'

'Much Wenlock way?'

'That's it. You come along with me and I'll show you the carriage. I'll be working on the holding. They'll take you on too if you like.'

'Very well,' I replied. 'I'll come along with you for a while.'

'That's nice of you, dearie. I'm staying on here till the day after tomorrow, so if you like you can move over here and share the hut with me, seeing as your friends are off tomorrow.'

'All right, I'll do that.'

'Have you got much with you?'

'Very little,' I replied promptly.

'Good. That'll make it easier travelling. See you here tomorrow, then.'

Why she should have asked me to travel with her is something I'm not sure about to this day. Perhaps she wanted someone with her when she faced her new employers, to plead her case, for at the heart of almost every mumper is a deep seated inferiority complex. Or perhaps she thought she could whip some of my goods, in which case I was going to take damn good care she did not.

I began to look forward to the next couple of days loath though I was in many ways to travel with her, and, what was worse, to share the hut. But I was forever seeking a wider horizon. The travelling life is hard, sometimes monotonous, but never boring or frustrating. Each day spent travelling has been worth a hundred times more to me than months spent working in an office.

I said goodbye to my Gypsy friends and left the wagon, and walked across the wet field towards the two tents and two wooden huts at the far end; the Gypsies never pitch near the mumpers. The damp grasses flicked round my ankles, and with every step I took I became more dubious about my forthcoming venture.

I brought with me a blanket, groundsheet, saucepan and frying pan, enamel mug and plate, cutlery, matches, a change of underclothes, toilet requisites, a supply of food – tea, sugar, several packets of dried soup, a few onions, potatoes, carrots, and milk. I had over six pounds in cash. I kept the notes in a small bag attached to a piece of string which I wore round my neck. And I had a supply of loose coins kept in a purse in my pocket.

There had been five wagons pitched in the field and now they were all gone. I and five mumpers were the only pickers left. They and some locals had finished stripping the last rows in the morning. The five, when I appeared on the scene, were busy cooking their midday meal.

Ma half raised an arm as she saw me approaching, by way of salutation, then pointed to one of the huts. 'Saluki's sleeping in that one. You put your things in here along with mine.'

I dumped my things on the floor and emerged with my cooking paraphernalia and food. Cooking was done in pots suspended from cranes, and on open ovens across which were spaced iron bars.

'What are you having to eat?' Ma asked, food being an absorbing topic of conversation with this crowd.

She was dressed almost entirely in black: ugly man's shoes, the leather split in several places, no stockings, a wide crumpled linen skirt, and a blouse draped with a wool shawl. A piece of black material was tied round her head, and this added to the sallow look of her small face. The face struck me as being somewhat curious, though none of the features was in any way remarkable. It gave me an impression of both old age and childhood.

'By the way,' I remarked, 'how many children have you got?'

'Children?' she said, with an air of puzzlement. 'I ain't got no children. What makes you think I have?'

'Well, I suppose because your name's Ma. People called that are usually mothers.'

'Ma's just my road name,' she said evasively. 'It don't mean nothing.'

'Would you like to know how I came by my name?' asked Saluki, who had been sitting silently by an oven listening to our conversation. 'I chose it myself. Years ago I heard someone use the word 'saluki' and I thought it was the most beautiful word I ever heard. That's what I'll call myself, I thought. I'd only just taken to the road – not many people knew my name. Later on I learnt that Saluki was the name of some kind of a dog. It was too late to change it again then, so everyone calls me Saluki.'

Three men came out of the tents which were pitched some distance from the huts. I had exchanged brief conversations with them in the fields.

Two of them were travelling together. Both were tramps and went by the names of Fish-fry and Len. They spent the winter months in London. Fish-fry was a big, heavily built tramp, bearded, with grizzled white hair which flared out from under an old trilby. Len was a tiny man who spoke with a cockney accent. His face was covered with a dark stubble.

The third man was a disconsolate-looking Pole. He was quite young and travelled the roads alone.

'Care for some peas?' asked Fish-fry, taking a large paper bag from a pocket.

'Thanks, I could do with some,' said Ma. 'I didn't keep none when we was picking this morning.'

I dropped a handful of sliced potatoes into my frying pan.

'Watch how Fish-fry does his chips,' Len bade me. 'He works in chipperies most winters. That's how he came by his name.' The expert sliced his potatoes on to an enamel plate and then slid the lot into a none-too-clean handkerchief.

'That's the trick,' he informed me. 'Get them well dried off afore you put them into the pan. Stops 'em spluttering away like yours and keeps 'em nice and crisp. And there's got to be blue smoke coming off the fat afore you put them in.'

Len folded a length of paper and stuck it under a smouldering stick in order to draw the fire nearer his end. Everyone seated round the fire donated a couple of spoons of tea, and the leaves were put into a big iron kettle which had been borrowed from the farm. Saluki stirred the bubbling water with a stick until it was a deep reddish-brown. Then she poured a measure of this potion into our mugs. Everybody had his or her own supply of milk.

With a fork, Fish-fry pointed to the lone figure of the Pole who was sitting some yards from us, gulping from a bottle of beer.

'What's he think he is – an alcoholic anonymous?'

'Drowning his sorrows, by the looks o' things,' said Len with a trace of envy. An almost palpable aura of gloom emanated from this personage.

'His name's Sergei something or other,' said Ma.

'Come over here,' ordered Fish-fry.

Obediently, the Pole came over. Taking the bottle from him, Fish-fry downed the contents by several inches. We waited for the flare-up, but the Pole only smiled sadly and said nothing.

'Been and visited London?' asked Len in an attempt to draw him into the conversation.

'Zumtimes.'

'Have an idea I saw you once in the reading room of Aldgate Public Library?'

The Pole said nothing, then just as conversation was starting up again, he suddenly burst out with – 'Before the war my home was in Wroctaw, in South Poland.'

'Was it now?' said Fish-fry indifferently, removing the chips from his pan and putting in some halved tomatoes and sausages in their place. 'Never fry anything else with chips – spoils their flavour and makes them soft and gooey.'

'Yes,' said the Pole with a deep sigh. 'I was engaged to a Jewish girl. Before the Germans walk into Poland I take a ship to South America – I was a sailor. And while there I hear of the disaster that has overtaken my country. . .'

'Anybody got any mustard?' queried Fish-fry. 'It adds a bit of zip to the sausages. No? Well, I'll just have to eat 'em without any.'

'I come to England, and after the war I find out she has died in a concentration camp – she, and all her family. Since I heard that news I have taken many jobs and lived in many different places. I have stayed in men's hostels, rooms, a small flat, but I do not stay anywhere for long. Since I heard of her death. . .' His voice trailed away and his glance went from face to face, as though he were searching for some look of response that would draw him from the lonely world his past seemed to have committed him to, and back into the stream of communal life. But none of us was able or willing to give him the response he sought, and for the rest of the meal he sat with lowered head, saying nothing, his fingers plucking at the grasses. Later that day he packed up his things and left.

In the evening I went over to the farm to buy some eggs. I had a brief wash under a tap by a cattle trough, then I walked back in the semi-darkness to the hut. The door was closed. I pushed it open and lit a candle stump, sticking it upright in a pool of grease on the floor. Ma was already asleep. I had a quick check of my belongings. Nothing missing so far. The hut was quite bare of furniture except for a wooden bench which ran the length of one wall. Three hooks protruded from the walls, and there was a small trade mirror under them stamped with the brand of a popular cigarette.

I combed and brushed my hair and laid out my bedding. My entry and the flare of the candle had not caused Ma to stir at all. She lay, fully clothed, against a wall, a piece of canvas under her, a length of blanket on top, while her head rested on a bag containing her few belongings.

The flame of the candle gyrated as thin gusts of air assailed it through cracks in the walls. Presently Ma shifted her position slightly. She muttered something, then said, strangely: 'Don't play that tune again: – it's crossed with violets. . .' The words were spoken softly but audibly, and disturbed the air like the wings of moths.

I opened the door a fraction to ease the foetid atmosphere caused by the old woman's unwashed person and clothing. The candle went out with a faint hiss. I lay down in the dark, pulling the blanket up round my head. A light rain drummed on the tarmac roof. It was very cold in the hut after the warm wagon I had slept in the night before, but in spite of the chill I was soon asleep.

The next morning, having collected our pay from the farmer, Ma and I set off together in a south-easterly direction. I soon began to have doubts whether the old railway wagon she said she was making for existed except in her imagination. I was indifferent whether we ever reached it. I was quite free to leave her at any time – in an hour, a day, or a week, just whenever I pleased.

To me, the tramps and mumpers are the nomadic escapers from life.

The majority of them take to the roads because they are fleeing from various personal problems. As I wandered along the roads with Ma, some words of the young Russian émigré Isabelle Eberhardt, came to my mind. She died in Algeria at the age of twenty-seven, and her strange, brief life was largely spent in a passionate search for freedom.

'All property has its bounds,' she had written, 'and all power is subject to some law, but the humble nomad possesses the whole vast earth, whose only limits are the unreal horizon, and his empire is intangible since he governs it and enjoys it in spirit.'

Her words are true in a sense, but they do not apply to a person who has taken to the nomadic life as a means of escaping from some problem. If he does so he will certainly not possess the whole vast earth, and a nomadic existence will merely act as a palliative to his ills, for essentially freedom lies in the mind. Such things as keeping one's possessions to a minimum, travelling about the countryside, rendering up any power one may possess, do not necessarily bring a greater freedom, though they may help to do so if one has at least experienced a few moments, had a glimpse of a freer life and from there has gone on to widen the sphere of freedom. Then, if one feels one must give a reason, to oneself or others, for living what must be deemed a somewhat strange existence in contemporary society, one can use the word 'freedom' in all sincerity and not the word 'escape'.

The old woman did not make any demands on my company. We seldom spoke as we walked, and I could think my own thoughts.

What, I wondered, had made her take to the life of the roads? When we did exchange a few words they were seldom about the past or the future, but referred to some scene or object which had caught our attention; a tethered goat, a white rooster perched on a gate, fields of peas with no pickers in view. I left the task of route finding entirely to her. She hardly glanced at a signpost and seemed to take a particular road more by instinct than because of a direct knowledge that it would lead in a certain direction.

'Inside the railway wagon is a spring bed and two chairs. At one end there's a fireplace,' she said, as we ate fried tomatoes, bread and bacon during a midday halt. 'The weather was quite cold the last time I was there and so I used to go out and collect sticks for the fire. It's one of the best places I've ever been to – you'll see.'

Would I?

'How far away is it now?' I asked.

'Only a couple of days' walking.'

'What! But you said before we left the farm that it would only be a day and a half's walk and already we've been —'

'No, no, I'm wrong,' she said hurriedly. 'We'll get there tomorrow midday. If we don't then we'll take a lift.'

'If we don't I'll be leaving you,' I said.

'Don't leave before we get there,' she begged.

I said nothing as I cut another slice of bread and dropped it into the pan, then I took out a pencil and notebook from a pocket.

'What's that you're writing down?' she asked suspiciously.

'A list of the things I'm going to buy in the next village.'

'Well, you don't have to write them down. What you got a brain for?'

FOUR

The Hermit

ALL MY BONES, since I had started picking, had begun to creak. The stiffness of my body had been made worse by the damp, drizzly weather of the past few days. The previous night Ma and I had slept in a barn in which square bales of straw were stacked at one end and a pile of loose hay had made a comfortable mattress. But in spite of having my blanket and groundsheet on top of me I had shivered most of the night and slept little. A damp, cold air had blown in through the wide entrance of the barn. In the early hours of the morning a pale sun had risen and the hedges started to steam. I laid out my spare clothing on a tractor to give them an airing. My fingers were so stiff and curled that they might have been an old woman's. It was minutes before they became supple, and I had difficulty in opening a tin of beans and preparing breakfast. No wonder so many tramps are the victims of rheumatism, I thought.

No doubt I too would succumb to the disease should I continue this way of life much longer.

When not travelling I give a certain amount of attention to my diet. I eat a salad a day, seldom open a tin, cut down on fried foods and drink fresh fruit juice. This healthy diet comes to a stop when I am with travellers. The Gypsies as a whole do not eat badly at all, though they are inclined to eat too much tinned and starchy food these days. But the tramps and mumpers must be among the world's unhealthiest eaters. It is less a question of their having little money than simply having no idea of what constitutes a healthy diet, or simply not caring what they eat nor how they cook their food. About the only 'fresh' food they eat regularly is potatoes. These are fried, along with a strip of bacon, or sausage, or tomato. Whenever they spend money on food it always goes on tins of baked beans, sausages, condensed milk, packets of tea, white sugar, white bread, and cheap cakes. Everything is fried. Sometimes for days on end they live on nothing but cups of strong tea and fried potatoes. Fruit and fresh greens seem to appeal little to their taste, although they can get them during the summer months free or for next to nothing. It is no wonder that many of them appear sickly and undernourished, and where not suffering from some definite disease are seldom in robust good health.

As we were clearing up the lunch things and stamping out the fire, a local man passed by and asked what we were about.

'Strange as it may seem to you,' I said, 'we have just eaten lunch and are now packing up to go on. We're pickers. Any more questions?'

'I reckoned you were pickers,' he said, lighting a cigarette and apparently all set for a gossip. 'Ever been up there?' he asked, and pointed to a line of trees in the distance.

'No,' I said, wiping round the frying pan with a piece of bread. 'Who lives there?'

'Our local hermit. Lives in a big house all by himself and never comes out. Just puts a hand outside the door for his milk bottle and week's groceries. There's a wall running round the house, all the lower windows are barred, and the front and back doors are kept bolted. All the years he's been there only two people have ever seen him. They were a couple of young lovers. They were sitting on top of the wall, holding hands and talking, when suddenly the girl says, 'There's a man standing at the window looking at us!' And sure enough, there he was – the hermit! Gave them quite a turn. There was something very queer about him – it made them jump down from the wall and run off.'

'And what did he look like?' I asked.

'He had a beard, kind of piercing eyes, he was tall, and wore a zipped jacket and brown corduroy trousers.'

'What made him go and live there like that?'

'Nobody knows. He's been living there now for about twelve years. Nuts, if you ask me. Quite a lot of the local people go prowling round the place to see if they can get a look at him, but so far only that young couple have seen him.'

We talked for a while longer, then he walked off. But instead of putting her things together, Ma said: 'I don't feel like going on yet. It's nice and sunny now. I think I'll have a nap.'

'Very well,' I said. 'I'll go and have a look at the hermit and then come back here.'

'You'll be wasting your time if you think you'll get a look at him. He keeps himself hidden, and I don't blame him.'

'I'll go just for the walk.'

'Very well. Expect you when I see you,' and she lay down and closed her eyes.

When I had walked across the field I came upon a boy pulling an old bird's nest out of the hedge.

'Where are you going?' he asked.

'I'm going to have a chat with the hermit,' I replied.

'I thought you were one of them mumper types when I first saw you. You don't live round about here, do you?'

'No, I don't,' I said.

'Who told you about the hermit?'

'Aha!'

'Do you know where his house is?'

'Somewhere over there,' I said.

'I'll show you. I don't like going by myself, but I get a bit of a thrill if I go with someone else. Maybe we'll see him.'

The boy walked in front of me along the hedgerow. He had thick yellow hair which flopped about his head. I took him to be a farmer's child. We came to a short area of woodland sparsely dotted with trees and the ground covered with bluebells. 'Not far now,' he called back over his shoulder. A few yards from where the trees ended ran the wall which encircled the hermit's dwelling. The boy walked on to where the ground rose partly up the wall and, digging his plimsolled feet into cracks, started to climb up. I followed.

'There,' he said, as we sat on top of the wall with our legs hanging down the side, 'doesn't the place give you the creeps?'

There was something rather strange about the atmosphere. A curious silence hung about the place, brooding and watchful, seeming to emanate from the house itself. 'My name's Nicholas,' he said, throwing a stone on to the weed-grown area which surrounded the house. 'I'd never come here by myself – never! Nor would a good many other people I know.'

It is when one comes across a rare case like this hermit that one realises how gregarious human beings are, for why else should a man who for some reason has decided to live alone and cut himself off from others attract such curiosity and even a certain amount of unease? The house was tall, three storeys, and all the lower windows were barred and the panes so grimy that they appeared from a distance to be covered with a grey mist. We were at the rear of the building. On the other side ran a roadway, and I was surprised to note in myself a slight feeling of relief that traffic and pedestrians might pass by and make the atmosphere seem less pregnant with isolation.

'One thing I reckon I'd never have the guts to do,' the boy said.

'What's that?'

'Jump down and look through one of the windows – would you?'

I had to laugh. His question made me feel back in my childhood again, being dared to walk on forbidden and dangerous territory.

'I might,' I said. I was rather curious to take a look through a window now that he had mentioned it.

'Well, if you will, I will,' he said bravely. 'But promise me, if anything happens, you won't run off and leave me. And I promise not to run off and leave you. Right?'

'Right, I promise.' I slipped down on to the turf and Nicholas followed.

We walked towards the house. Once I bent down and picked up a rusty old tin, then put it back among the dandelions again. Everything here, one felt, was a little strange and out of the ordinary, even a tin. I found myself walking on tiptoe, quietly, speaking in a whisper, and I noticed that Nicholas automatically did the same. The deep silence seemed to be alive and increasing in watchfulness. We peered through a grey pane and saw nothing but a room, empty except for a wooden chair and a strip of carpet. We turned the handle of the back door – it was locked. Then we walked slowly round to the front of the house. The ground was nothing but patches of bare earth, with areas of grass and weeds and loose stones; not a flower or bush or flower bed to relieve the drab monotony and unkempt look.

The front door differed in no way from the back door. We tried the handle and pushed, but the door did not give, then we looked into another room through the iron bars and dirty glass. This room was totally devoid of furniture, there was not even a piece of carpet on the floorboards. We turned and started to go back.

I do not know exactly when it was that I realised we were being watched. My back was to the house, yet I knew for a certainty that someone was watching us, and with this knowledge came that queer spine-chilling feeling down my back.

The boy immediately sensed my uneasiness and asked, 'What's the matter?' Then he looked round. 'Oh, my God! The hermit's watching us.' With a bound he speeded away towards the wall and climbed it like a monkey. 'Come quick!' he yelled. 'Quick, what are you waiting for?'

I stood there for the simple reason that I could not go forward; something held me back, and then impelled me to return towards the window.

'Oh, please!' I heard an agonised cry in the distance. 'Don't go. . .'

I did not go right up to the window. I took a few paces towards it and then stopped. Staring at me was a man of medium height, clean-shaven, with a pale, rather pointed face. He was dressed in a white open-necked shirt and grey trousers, and his hands were stuck in his trouser pockets. The look he gave me was one I cannot forget. I returned his stare, and it was as if aeons separated us, worlds, vast stretches of space, yet in some tenuous fashion we contacted one another. If he had opened the window and put out a hand I could no more have touched it than I would willingly touch the hand of a corpse. Somehow I had the feeling that part of him had died; but his eyes were alive and were all the more compelling, perhaps, just because the rest of him had ceased to live.

Neither of us spoke; we just continued staring at one another, and the feeling grew in me that if he did not take his eyes off me soon I would not be able to get away and up that wall, and there was nothing I longed to do more during those moments he held me there. The situation, even then, struck me as somewhat ridiculous, for why should I be afraid? Afraid, I was. True, I had trespassed on his property. Even so, my fear went beyond any sense of guilt at having trespassed. Presently I found my voice.

'I am sorry,' I said, 'for having disturbed you.'

He did not move, no shade of expression appeared on his face. I did not know whether he had even heard my words, yet somehow I think he had.

I walked back to the wall, and as I reached the top my arm was seized by Nicholas. 'Oh, thank heavens,' he gasped. 'I thought you were never coming. Whatever made you stay?'

But without waiting for me to reply he jumped down from the wall and ran off through the trees. I only caught up with him when I came to the hedgerow. He was sitting down, a dazed expression on his face.

'Gosh, that was awful! I'm never going anywhere near that place.'

'Maybe that's a good thing,' I said. 'That house belongs to him and we shouldn't have gone prowling around looking through his windows.'

'What did you say to him? I heard you call out something.'

'I told him I was sorry for disturbing him – and I am.' And I still am, all these years later.

Ma was combing out a few bedraggled strands of hair when I returned to our luncheon spot.

'Well,' she asked, 'did you see him?'

'Yes, I did.'

'Yes. And I've just seen a man from Mars and Uncle Tom Cobley! Well, we'd better get moving.'

I had made up my mind to leave the old woman the following day as I did not believe we would ever find the wagon. But to my surprise, as we were walking along in the early afternoon, Ma suddenly announced that we were almost there. We walked down a lane bordered by a tall holly hedge in which small birds scuttled like mice. At the end of the lane was a red brick bungalow set in a large holding. We stopped by the gate and waited.

A woman was beating a carpet near a rhubarb patch. On seeing us, she laid down the beater and came towards us, brushing aside the tall leaves.

'May we put up in the wagon a while?' Ma asked politely. 'If you remember, I stayed here last year.'

'Yes, I remember,' said the woman in an expressionless voice. She had a heavy, thick-set body.

'We'd be obliged if you'd give us work in exchange for a few taters, milk and eggs and the loan of the wagon,' said Ma.

The woman studied me. 'What work can you do?'

'I can help about the holding or, if you prefer, I can help about the bungalow.'

'Very well. I'll see what I can find for you. Come this way. I'll give you the wagon key.'

After the great shadowy barn, where we had slept the night before, the wagon gave an impression of cosiness. It stood alongside a hedge and was some distance from the bungalow. It was approached through a grove of birch trees. Going up the wooden steps, I unlocked the door. The furniture consisted of a spring bed, on which was a grubby-looking mattress and blanket, two chairs, a table, a strip of lino on the floor, and an orange box for fuel. The last occupant had omitted to clean out the grate, which was filled with white ash. I cleaned it out, lit a fire, then returned to the bungalow.

'What made you take up with her?' the woman, a Mrs Braddock, asked me.

'She just happened to be going the same way as I was,' I replied. 'She told me about the railway wagon you have and that maybe you could give us work. That's what I've come down about – is there anything you want doing now?'

'All I want doing now is to have the eggs collected and the hens fed.'

'Very well.'

This job completed, I returned once more to the bungalow, and Mrs Braddock started to question me again.

'Where did you meet up with her?'

'At the last farm where I was working.'

'Were you there by yourself?'

'No, I was with some Gypsy friends. I slept in their wagon.'

'Gypsies. . .' she said, and a look of curiosity appeared on her sallow face. 'Can you tell fortunes?'

'Yes,' I answered.

When I live as a traveller I earn my living in the ways they do, though it is something of a labour of love where my fortune-telling, or dukkering, is concerned: I never accept any money when I read a palm or the tarot.

'How do you tell them?' she asked.

'By the palm, tarot pack, or crystal.'

'And how much do you charge?'

'Nothing.'

'Oh, but I'd be willing to pay you something.'

'Nothing,' I repeated.

I made this rule for myself – unfortunately – of accepting no fee the day I picked up my set of tarot cards for the first time. I give readings only to those I wish to and when I wish to. It is very necessary to retain one's freedom in this respect. Once one accepts money for a reading one is immediately under an obligation to the client to tell him something or other, when perhaps there is virtually nothing to tell, or what one sees would be better left unsaid.

There is one important fact which should be more widely known in regard to the telling of fortunes. In the normal way we can, if we are observant and alert, tell a great deal about a person by the expression, stance, build, way of speaking and so on; even the 'hidden' inclinations and desires often come through to us though the person may never voice them. When a seer is really gifted with a highly developed intuitive sense, then on studying a client's palm or gazing into the crystal he is given a deeper glimpse, as it were, into the client's intimate inner life. He immediately has an awareness, to a far greater degree than a normal contact would offer, into that person's character and leanings. He can 'see' the undeveloped potentialities, the strengths and weaknesses, the sexual inclinations. He may also see events, get flashes into the client's past or future life, realise the direction in which the personality is swinging. The majority of seers are no more shocked or elated by what they discover about their clients than is a physician when dealing with his patients' maladies. But every person has a right to withhold certain aspects of his private life from another should he wish it.

The clairvoyant cannot in all honesty pretend to see certain aspects of his client's life and not others; the good and the not-so-good reveal themselves with equal intensity. What he tells his client is only a small portion of what he sees. For a variety of reasons, he may withhold a great deal of what he has become aware. The benefit of a reading from a gifted seer is that a strong light is thrown on to the client's life, revealing himself more clearly to himself, the seer acting as the mirror. The recounting of past, present and future events is of secondary importance. What concerns the clairvoyant is how strong the light should be for each individual client; some persons can see themselves in a strong light without flinching, others can't.

At Mrs Braddock's request I said I would come down to the bungalow after the evening meal and read her duk. She gave me a pint of milk, some eggs, potatoes, and a slab of home-made cake.

That evening I cooked up a large tomato omelette while Ma cut and buttered slices of bread. Almost every day of late I had suffered from intermittent pangs of indigestion, and I realised that I would have to start a more healthy diet before long.

The repast over, Ma started to unroll the mattress. 'I think I'll take a cat-nap,' she said, yawning. 'All that walking's worn me out.'

She was always having a doze, always seemed tired, and her mind often drifted to shadowy realms.

'I'll meet him and Jenny tomorrow,' she had said that morning, apropos of nothing as we were walking along together.

'Meet who?' I had asked.

She had looked at me as though seeing me for the first time, and then said sharply, 'Don't interrupt. I was talking to someone else.'

As I got ready to leave the wagon she watched me like an anxious child. 'Where are you going?' she enquired.

'Down to the bungalow to see Mrs Braddock.'

'Didn't she ask me down too?'

'She asked me to go down and tell her fortune,' I said.

'Oh, I see. You can tell mine, too, when you get back. A Gypsy once told me I should do something with figures and give up picking. I don't know if she meant take up the pools or go in for an office job. But it was strange she said that. Arithmetic was always my best subject at school. Not that I could add two and two these days.'

Mrs Braddock and her husband were waiting for me in the bungalow sitting room. She was in a puce housecoat and he was in pyjamas and a green dressing gown.

'We always relax in the evenings,' she said. 'Just sit down and make yourself comfortable.'

Somewhat to my dismay, I saw a large quantity of food and a teapot on a trolley, and I wished I had not eaten such a big supper.

'Well, shall we begin?' asked Mrs Braddock. 'We'll have some tea and cakes later.'

I do not really care to dukker with a third person present. However, I started off; glanced at her left hand and read from the right. Short fate line, long, uninterrupted life line, islanded heart line, a faint sun line. Everything added up to a dull, uneventful life. No sooner had I finished reading her palm than her husband held out his hand.

When persons have allowed one to glimpse something of their private lives through a reading, they are then often willing to talk about themselves in a way they would never dream of doing otherwise; the barriers are down. As I ate cakes and sandwiches, washed down by several cups of tea, I listened to them telling incidents of their lives, their hopes, their failures. One would stop talking for a while to take a gulp of tea and the other would immediately continue the conversation.

'Can you read your own hand?' Mr Braddock asked me.

'Yes, I can give a straight reading,' I replied. 'But to give a true dukkering there must be a reflector – another human being. You can't be a reflector to yourself.'

My own life line is pronged at mid-youth – a double life line – and exactly represents events in my own life.

It was past twelve when I said goodnight to the Braddocks.

The wagon stood out black against the night sky. Although the hour was late I caught the sound of a frail tune coming from a radio in a distant cottage. I wound my way between the birch twigs. Ma's heavy, strained breathing greeted me as I pushed open the wagon door.

I felt as though I had only been in bed an hour when I woke at daybreak. Getting up, I dressed and lit a fresh fire outside the wagon, using a newspaper, candle stump and a few dry twigs to get it going. I filled the kettle and slung it on the crane. In spite of my clatter, Ma slept on heavily. I was halfway through cooking breakfast before she finally roused herself. She sat up, put a hand to her head as though trying to recollect where she was, then called out a faltering good morning.

It was during the brief moments of dawn that she was at her best. She was more at her ease then, and able to express her emotions more freely. Sometimes, as we sat eating breakfast, she would lay a hand on my knee and urge me to eat up, or cut me another slice of bread. When the sun rose and revealed her emaciation and defeat, her manner became somewhat furtive and touched with asperity. She became crippled, too, by an excessive timidity. Yet though negative emotions chained her for the greater part of each day, perception assured me it was her truer self that was released at dawn.

Later that morning, on returning from the holding, where I had been weeding between rows of young onion plants, I found Ma sitting in the yard staring dreamily ahead of her, her arms sunk in a pail of soapy water. Mrs Braddock was watching her from a window.

'She's not done a stroke of work these past five minutes,' she called out to me. 'I asked her to wash down those reed mats.'

'I'll wash them,' I said.

I looked at Ma. Physical and mental energy ran through her at a low ebb. She drew her arms from out of the pail and started to rub a mat slowly with a piece of cloth.

'I'll tell your fortune this evening, Ma,' I said.

At these words, she came to with surprising suddenness.

'You try!' she said, in a voice which shook with mingled bitterness and hatred. She glared at me in silence for a moment, then muttered, 'You're worse than my mother.'

'In what way,' I asked, 'am I worse than her?'

'No,' she said at once, 'I didn't really mean that. You're not.' Her expression became milder.

'But why,' I persisted, 'did you speak like that about your mother?'

She paused before answering and then said, almost in spite of herself, 'Before I was born she and father used to say, 'Third time lucky.' Their first two children were both girls. They wanted a boy, and they got me. Later, Mother used to tell me that if it had been possible she'd have liked to get me adopted or sent to a children's home. . .'

'Did she really tell you that?'

'Oh, yes, she often used to tell me that.'

I decided to change the subject. 'In what sort of a house did you live as a girl?'

'A council house. It was always kept very clean and neat. Respectable, that's what the neighbours used to call us. You wouldn't have recognised me in those days. I kept very neat and respectable myself as a young woman. Every evening I used to rinse out my undies and hang them over the rail to dry. I'd give myself a wash all over and say my prayers before I got into bed. I never lacked for anything in the way of food or clothing. One day I decided I just couldn't stand life at home any longer. It was just that. . . no, I can't explain, but I just couldn't stand it. I packed a suitcase, sneaked out of the house and caught a train for Birmingham. I managed to get a job in an office there, but they didn't keep me long. I wasn't trained for office work. I wasn't trained for anything, come to that, except housework which I'd been doing at home. They gave me the sack after a short while.'

'And then?'

'Then I got a job in a factory. But my health started to go. I couldn't stand factory life, anyway. I got one or two jobs Birmingham way, but each one got worse. So I took to the road. I tried a few times to get back to a settled life but I never made it. . . Well, it's too late now.'

She relapsed into silence, and I finished cleaning the mats.

The following morning when I rose from my hard bed on the floor I noticed that the spring bed was empty. I looked through a window but could not see Ma about anywhere. Then I saw that her few belongings were not in the wagon. She had got up, packed, and left without waking me or saying goodbye. I left too that same day, but I did not meet up with Ma again.

FIVE

Solitary Wandering

T HE DAY after Ma and I had parted company, I set off in the direction
of the Clee Hills. I had decided to walk during the coming night and
sleep the following morning.

I enjoy travelling at night when the weather is fine. It seems a pity
to me that man is so much a creature of the day and grows ever more
so with the march of civilisation. The spirit which is abroad at night is
different from the spirit of the daylight hours and should be experienced
every so often. Owing to climatic conditions, it is the people of the East
who are, and ever have been, more knowledgeable and appreciative
of the hours when the moon rules the heavens. Many easterners still
sleep without the barrier of roofs under the brilliant stars, and do much
travelling at night in order to avoid the heat of the day. Because they are
not strangers to the countryside at night one does not encounter in them

the same fear and unease of the nocturnal hours which one frequently does in the West.

I had supper in a small inn, then started off again with a packet of freshly cut sandwiches and my thermos filled with hot coffee.

The moon was ahead of me, a clear silver orb, but her light did not dim the galaxy of stars. I remembered the saying: 'The wise man rules his stars; the fool is ruled by his,' and searched the heavens for familiar groups and single stars – the Ram, the Bull, the Heavenly Twins, the blue star Sirius, Cassiopeia and the Pole Star.

The country was composed of open, hillocky fields, and copses. I entered a lane. An occasional cottage stood back from it. Most of the dwellings I passed were in darkness, their inhabitants gone to bed. In a few the lights were still shining. Before much longer, I thought, it is probable that I shall be the only person awake under the open skies in this stretch of countryside. All the rest will be asleep, dreaming, oblivious of the beauty of the night.

A signpost stood up whitely in the distance. I read the names of the hamlets to which its arms pointed. There was sufficient light to read them without the light of my torch. This was the only occasion on the night's walk that I followed a signpost's direction. For the rest of the way I took a glance now and then at my compass and the Pole Star in order to check that I was continuing in a more or less southerly direction. There is an anonymous quality about the night which makes me take even less note of the names of places I pass through than I do during the day.

I came to another crossroads. After I had walked a short distance I suddenly felt an urge to turn round. I did so, and saw the figure of a man standing at the crossing watching me. For the space of a few seconds we stood staring at one another. His face was a pale blur; I could see nothing of its features. As I watched him he turned and walked away. I did not see another person throughout the rest of the night.

The lane dropped between high banks, on the tops of which were stunted hawthorn bushes. Coming to a gate, I climbed over it, and found myself among another group of open, grassy hills. As I walked along the hilltops, the moon before me, it looked at times as though it were only a few brief yards away and that the extension of an arm would be almost sufficient to enable me to touch the orb's lower rim. Then a vaporous, russet cloud would be blown across the moon's face, bringing perspective, by which I gained a faint apprehension of the vast spaces which separated it from the earth.

I sat down on a rock. All around me were hills and dark hollows in which perhaps lay houses and villages. Not far ahead was the black, straggling shape of a wood. The sky was a deep, vivid blue, and it seemed to impart a silence on the land lying below. The grasses bent, but the wind which swung them moved silently. Out of this quietness came two of the loneliest sounds I know. First, the distant whistle of a train, long drawn-out and lingering, as it sped across the countryside. And shortly after the sound had died away came the hoot of an owl from somewhere in the wood beyond.

In spite of a loaded haversack, walking was effortless. It must be purely imagination, but I always feel that the law of gravity is less exigent at night, particularly when the moon's rays are strong.

On approaching the wood, I decided not to skirt it but to continue straight on into its depths and trust that they did not extend any great distance.

The darkness under the trees after the moonlit countryside was intense. I halted a minute to give my eyes time to adjust themselves to the surrounding blackness. For some reason I felt reluctant to switch on my torch. Slowly I began to walk on, one hand extended to ward off branches, the other held against my face. I was constantly tripping over roots and bramble trailers and soon began to wish that, instead of plunging recklessly into its depths, I had skirted the wood, even if this had meant going several miles off my course. I deliberated whether or not to turn back, but having come so far it seemed foolish not to continue forwards.

My head met with the heavily leafed branch of an elder tree. I felt the shapes of the leaves and listened to the silence, a silence utterly different from that which pervaded the open country. This one was brooding and forbidding and I longed for it to be broken by the flutter of wings or scurrying feet of some woodland creature, anything that was warm and alive. But nothing stirred. The only sound I could hear was that of my own rapid breathing. Atavistic fears were gaining hold of my mind, try though I did to suppress them, menacing and nameless, yet the more frightening just because I did not know exactly what I feared. Although I realised that it would do nothing to calm me – in fact probably add to my growing panic – I switched on the torch. I looked nervously around at the dark wall composed of trunks and branches, and I had the feeling of being trapped.

Hurriedly, I switched off the torch. Fear was now running through me like an electric current. I was quite incapable of making a getaway from the wood either by doubling back on my tracks or going forward. Overcome with terror, it was as much as I could do to crawl under the branches of the elder, where, slumped on my knees, I clung to its trunk, my eyes tightly closed. Goodness knows how long I would have remained in this ignominious position or what condition my mind would have been in had the feeling of helpless terror lasted much longer. But there then occurred a small incident which dispelled this aura of fear, emanating from my own mind, almost in a flash. Fond as I am of all wild creatures, it has seldom been my good fortune to be accepted at once by bird or beast as a friend except on a few rare occasions. This was one of them.

As I crawled under the branches I must have disturbed a bird in its sleep, but instead of flying off with startled cries, it fluttered down on to my shoulder. Judging from its weight, it might have been a blackbird or thrush. Soon enough it must have realised that it had perched on a living human being. This knowledge, however, did not seem to disturb it, for it remained on my shoulder some little time, fluttered a wing and uttered a sleepy chirp before flying back to its perch among the leaves. My terror evaporated and I continued on my way through the wood.

Strange as those fears seem to me now, the memory of those panic-stricken minutes have made me conscious of what people mean when they speak of going mad through fear.

The trees thinned out gradually and I saw the moon again. The illuminated hands of my watch pointed to ten past two. I was beginning to feel hungry, so I ate a couple of sandwiches and poured myself a mug of coffee from the thermos.

Another hour's walk brought me to a narrow, rough road which led down to a village.

All the lights were out, no cat mewled on a roof. I found myself tiptoeing through the deserted streets. I sat down on a bench, walked round the duck pond, and inspected an old felt hat someone had discarded near the Bull and Feathers. The moon was now at her brightest and the inn sign could be easily read at quite a distance.

Eventually I came to a church. Moonlight struck a blue haze off the stonework and the white marble crosses marking the graves. Squeezing through the wicket gate, I strolled along the gravelled paths. Unclipped yews cast shadows on the grass, darker than their own dark foliage. A lime tree filled the air with scent. Under glass domes the white china flowers, which hitherto I had regarded as meretricious offerings to the dead, now appeared strangely beautiful. The white flower bunches had a transparency and faery quality under the blue skies of night. I read an inscription on a small marble cross. Annie . . . four years and three months. A single pink tulip in a jam jar was set on her grave.

I lay down on a flat tombstone and watched the night slowly merge into dawn. Most of the stars had vanished. The moon was the colour of watered milk, her light almost gone.

Birds began twittering in the dense yews, and from the distance came the sound of a sheep coughing. A glow shone in the east. Later, from far off, came man-made sounds of buckets being slapped down on stone and someone calling to another.

I glanced at my watch – a quarter past five.

Leaving the churchyard, I walked along a lane until I reached a hazel spinney. The ground was covered with wild onion plants and the green heads of sorrel. I breakfasted to a loud chorus of birds. Throwing them my crumbs, I tied a dark handkerchief round my head to keep the light from my eyes, and lay down to sleep. The day was just beginning.

The following morning I went by a series of local buses to Worcester, where I took a bath, had my clothes disinfected and bought some fresh underwear and a new blouse. I had a free week ahead of me which I was looking forward to, before I plunged back once again into the world of travellers.

I hitched into Evesham. I had no particular plan in mind as to how I was going to spend the remaining free days before starting on the local picking season. I walked down Evesham's main street, taking a glance into the shop windows. It was mid week and though there were a good many townspeople about I saw few travellers. Saturday is the one recognised off-day of the week that the farmer gives his hired labour, with Sundays free too if there is no urgent rush to get a crop in. The women pickers spend Saturday mornings marketing and often join the men in the pubs afterwards.

I had almost reached the bridge at the lower end of the town when the driver of a small lorry, seeing me walking along with my pack, called out that he could take me half way to Cheltenham. I accepted his offer of a lift. A day in Cheltenham seemed a good idea. I could leave my pack at the station, and then go the round of small antique shops in search of a few pieces of gold jewellery of the kind admired by the Romany women. I knew I could chop any such pieces later on and make some good bargains. Gold jewellery is much worn and admired by these women.

The driver of the lorry dropped me off at a main crossroads. It was a warm and brilliant day. A signpost pointed away from the main road to a village called Teddington. I hesitated, watching the traffic as it sped by a few feet away. So be it. I would go to Teddington instead.

A minute off the busy main road and I was in the country. It did not take me long to reach the lovely little village of Teddington, with its timbered and thatched cottages and old church. But I did not stay there long, for over to the right of the village was a hill which had arrested my attention. Part of it was covered with woodlands and part with well-tended, lofty orchards, the serried ranks of cultivated fruit trees making a pleasant contrast to the wild woods. The summit of the hill was open country, and I could make out the shapes of horses and cattle grazing on its heights. Seeing this hill I felt it to be special, a hill in a thousand, and so indeed it proved to be. I had no map with me and only learnt later that it is called Oxenton Hill.

Climbing through a gap in the hedge, I started to make my way towards it over some meadows. The ground rose slowly, the meadows giving way to open country covered with furze and bramble bushes. Some minutes of steady climbing brought me to the woodlands, and I was struck by the variety and beauty of the trees. Winding round about them were narrow tracks imprinted with the hooves of cattle. Emerging from the woodlands there stretched before me slopes of lush, bright green meadowlands and, beyond them, orchards. Here, in these meadows, the trees were even more beautiful. Most grew singly, some in small groups – crab apple, pollard willow, aspen, and many others. Running down the hillside was a stream almost hidden by thick grasses and flowers. Here and there it widened out into little pools. Cows grazed contentedly, hardly bothering to raise their heads as I passed, and sheep and horses were grazing further up the hill. A breeze swept these upland meadows, blowing out manes and tails. With each step I took the view became more lovely.

Directly I walked under the trees I knew that I had discovered an enchanted piece of countryside.

When I reached the summit and looked over to my right, I saw stretched out, below and beyond, a miniature prairie over which horses galloped freely. At the far end of the prairie – which might comprise about five acres – was a farmhouse. The top of the hill and its environs was composed of scrubland, meadows and small copses. I walked the length of this English prairie and found that it ended in steep, cliff-like decline. In the distance was the main road with its steady flow of traffic. Immediately below me was another lovely village, the village of Oxenton. Here, on this lofty and luminous hill I resolved to stay until I went picking. But before I spread my groundsheet there was the question of a food supply to be fixed. I hid my pack under some bushes and set off down the steep hillside, past the church and through the village.

I spent the afternoon in Cheltenham buying food, candles and matches, and a small library of cheap books. A greengrocer gave me a sack and I bundled my purchases into this and took a bus back to Oxenton.

I made my camp in the woodlands some way below the summit. During the day I spread my groundsheet over the branches of a tree to form a temporary shelter in which to read and write up my notes. I lit my fire in a hollow space of the ground so as to avoid the danger of it spreading. Only twice during the following seven days did I leave the hill in order to buy more food and see something of the neighbouring villages and countryside.

Each day I walked my small domain and became ever more engrossed in the life of slopes and plateau. There was nearly always a breeze blowing up here and the atmosphere was invigorating. I felt I was at one with the life of the countryside, as much part of it as the animals and trees. And I was no longer conscious of the passing of time; there was no race to keep up with it nor periods of boredom when I waited for the slow minutes to tick by. I spent hours lying on the grass watching the clouds floating overhead. I observed the animals as they grazed. I picked bunches of sorrel and dandelion leaves to eat with my bread – I cut down cooking to the minimum. I also read a good deal.

All the literature I had bought in Cheltenham were books I had read before: Grey Owl's *The Men of the Last Frontier*, George Borrow's *Lavengro* and *Wild Wales*. I had a volume of Thomas Traherne's poems. His words, 'To sing in silence and to reign alone', often came to me while I was on the hill. I also had volumes of Emily Bronte's and Blake's poetry. All these writers, in their different ways, had been free spirits, living fully, quietly and adventurously. None had been tied to any cruel or rigid dogma.

Another writer who impressed me was Isabelle Eberhardt. I had read a brief account of her life in a magazine when I was a child, and I had decided to take several leaves from her notebook. Her early habit of corresponding with people in the overseas countries which interested her most – Algeria and Tunisia – I thought an excellent idea, and I decided to do some corresponding myself. My first pen-friend, not inappropriately, was an Arabian youth who hailed from the Yemen and was then living in Aden. I was to meet him years later in Tangier, and I am still in touch with him.

Before long I was writing to another correspondent, a Greek sailor. Like so many Britons, I have always felt a deep love for everything Grecian, though I have not yet visited Greece, nor have I yet met this correspondent. Part of Greece's attraction for me stems from that country's love of freedom and beauty.

A Hindu girl living in south India was another of my correspondents, and there were several others to whom I wrote more or less regularly.

During part of each day while I was camping at Oxenton, I sat near the summit of the hill where the grass was cropped short by the roaming sheep. And I thought of the great wind of the Reformation which had blown through these Islands centuries back and helped to deliver Europe from the superstitions and terrors of medievalism. With the coming of the Reformation religion was released from the straitjacket of Roman tyranny, and British genius burst into a wonderful flowering and transcended the fettered consciousness of a bygone age.

Names came and went through my head as I lay stretched out on the grass: John Wycliffe, whose body, burned by the public executioners, told the humble peasants of Leicestershire that the hand of the Pope could still reach the grave. Montrose, a man a few centuries in advance of his times – beheaded. And that last name brought to mind another, the Duke of Monmouth.

'Brave, beautiful, unfortunate. Aimed at a Crown but met his Fate.' On Tower Hill, to be precise. The words I have quoted are written on a painting of him by an unknown artist which now hangs in the National Portrait Gallery. He was 'the beloved Protestant Duke', the eldest of Charles II's fourteen acknowledged bastards. But there is reason to think that Monmouth was in fact legitimate and that Charles in his youth had contracted a form of marriage with his mother, Lucy Walter. This is a mystery surrounding his life.

I thought of some words he had written during a happy period of his life when he was living with his mistress, Henrietta Wentworth, in Holland. The words reflected my own feelings whilst I was living on Oxenton Hill. 'I am now so much in love with a retired life that I am never like to be found making a bustle in the world again.'

One night there was a thunderstorm which only lasted a few minutes. Lightning flashed above the branches and thunder reverberated around the hill. I heard the pounding of hooves in the distance as horses galloped for shelter. Rain spattered down on the leaves, but I remained dry. When it had stopped raining, a wind got up and soughed through the trees. It was a melancholy sound which seemed to bear within it all the sorrow of past centuries. And this sighing and sobbing of the wind continued until dawn.

I got up early. After breakfast I broke up the remains of a loaf into large pieces and distributed these to some sheep with whom I was by now on friendly terms, and who accepted my occasional offerings of bread with apparent relish.

The time had come for me to leave Oxenton Hill, with its diverse scenery, its trees, flowers, orchards and running streams, its peacefully grazing animals and its radiant solitude.

SIX

Travelling in Company

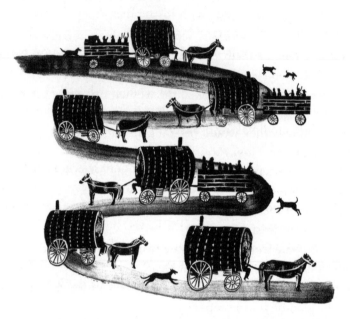

O N THE DUMBLETON ROAD back to Evesham I met up with one of the largest groups of wagons travelling together that I have yet come across; six horse-drawn wagons in all, together with three open traps crammed with Romany women and their chavvies and pet dogs running under or alongside the wagons. The caravanserai passed me, but I caught up with it again later, where the group had made a temporary pitch on open ground by the roadside. I saw my chance of continuing towards Warwickshire in company, gleaning news and gossip of the travelling fraternity.

In the travelling life one cannot wait for introductions, and so I walked towards the assembled group. An elderly woman, her head tied round with a scarf, was breaking up sticks and feeding them to the yog.

'Will you call the dogs off, mother?' I shouted, stepping in her direction and then halting as several large monsters started towards me.

At the sound of a stranger's voice every Gypsy, from the smallest toddler to the most elderly, left off what they were doing and looked at me with searching, penetrating eyes.

'Will you call the dogs off?' I repeated to the company at large. A man gripped a pair of them by the necks. They stood there growling ferociously. I walked round them.

'What d'you want, dearie?' asked the woman I had first addressed.

'You going Evesham or Stratford way?'

It seemed unlikely they would be going any other way.

'We're going up by Honeybourne.'

'That's my way,' I said promptly. 'I'm meeting up with Dan and Kizer Boswell nearby Stratford.'

'Never heard of them, dearie. We ain't going that far.'

'You come from Bristol?'

'Some of us come from Bristol, some from Pontypool, and some from the Forest.' (She meant the Forest of Dean.)

'I was wondering whether you'd let me travel with you as far as you're going. I'd be glad of your company.'

I was by now surrounded by Romanies. They appeared quite friendly, though in no great hurry to have me accompany them.

'We aren't reaching Honeybourne till tomorrow,' a man said, 'and the wagons are full.'

'That's all right. I have a blanket and groundsheet with me. I won't trouble you for sleeping quarters, but I should appreciate a lift, and I should like to stay over till the morning. Honeybourne, or nearabouts, will suit me fine. It'll be easy to get to Evesham from there. I want to buy a kipsie (basket) at a shop I know.'

'You don't want to make a special trip to Evesham, love, just to buy a kipsie. We have plenty here. Fetch some kipsies, Wincenty.'

Several children bounded off.

'What sort of kipsie do you want?' the crone questioned.

'A big one for hawking.'

'Well, we have plenty of those. You won't find a better one in Evesham. What do you hawk?'

'Plenty of things. When I meet up with the Boswells I'll be making paper flowers – they're always popular. I can give a dukkerin too.'

'You look as if you can, dearie.'

'Is them the Boswells who have a daughter called Thurzie?'

'That's right.'

'Where do they come from?'

'Right the other side of Wales. They used to deal a lot in horses and logs, but now they make most of their cash from picking.'

'Yes, you don't make much from horses and logs these days. Is that girl Thurzie married yet?'

'No, she's still thinking about getting married.'

'She's leaving it late, ain't she? What age is she getting on for?'

'Around nineteen.'

What looked remarkably like a great-great-grandmother pointed a finger at me.

'If a woman don't have her first baby afore she's twenty-one,' she said, 'then she's going to have a hard time when she does. That's what these young women don't seem to reckon with, and that's what their mothers should keep on telling them. Now Lisha here had her first child just four months back, no trouble at all and her only seventeen or thereabouts. If she'd waited till she was twenty-one or maybe more, things wouldn't have gone so good. I've seen some terrible cases with older women and all because they didn't get married young. You just tell that Thurzie when you see her. And now we'd better be eating. Choose your kipsie after we've ate. You can come along with us to Honeybourne.'

'That's kind of you.'

'You're welcome.'

The two basic meals of the day for Romanies are breakfast and supper. They often go without lunch if they are travelling or if the women have not made enough money from hawking to buy sufficient food for three meals. When travelling, little or no cooking is done at midday. A kettle is boiled up for tea and the families make do with bread, cheese and any leftovers. In the evening the big iron pots are suspended from the cranes and a good meal is cooked up.

That day I made do with buttered bread and a banana, and shared the Gypsies' tea. After this light repast, the Gypsies having eaten little more than I, the goods and chattels were gathered together, the fire stamped out, and we moved onwards. I sat in one of the traps along with three other women and four children. One of the children held a rope, to the other end of which was tied a young horse not yet broken in to the shafts. Two of the women had blonde hair and the other was a betwixt and between mouse.

One of the many misconceptions concerning British Romanies is that the majority of them have blue-black locks. Their hair is in the same colour range as the British gorgio. Black is probably the rarest shade met with amongst the Romanies, with the exception of those who spring from the fair and show folk, many of whom have Latin blood in their veins. It is the skin of the Romanies which has a dark hue, a deep tan, owing to the outdoor life they lead. One of the young women in the trap had plaited her blonde hair in two coils over her ears, Gypsy style, and a blonde child sat with a puppy in her lap, her hair hanging loose.

It would be a prejudiced person indeed who did not admit that Gypsy children have great charm. They are spontaneous, alert, good conversationalists, and though sometimes shy are lacking in self-consciousness. It is very seldom that one meets with an unhappy or neurotic child among the Gypsies, though with other travellers this is not always the case. If the Romany child survives infancy he is usually strong and healthy. A sickly person in this life is at a great disadvantage.

The first thing that strikes one when one lives for any length of time in a Gypsy community is that most Gypsies – except in the cases where much intermarrying has occurred – are emotionally whole. From the day of their birth to old age they are one of a community in which they are vitally interested. The children might be considered spoilt to the non-Gypsy way of thinking. If the chavvies are sometimes in need of warmer clothes and more adequate meals they never lack for human affection. Whereas the gorgio parent does everything he can to get his child as early as possible into a good school, the Gypsy parents to this day do everything in their power to keep their children out of school. Their efforts in this direction naturally have the child's approval.

One of the causes contributing to the Gypsy child's emotional stability and maturity is the fact that he lives throughout his life with persons of all ages and both sexes. He does not experience the sex segregation of boarding schools and the complete break with family life this entails for the greater part of each year. From an early age he knows the major facts of human life. Quite young girls may assist at births, and the older children take charge of the younger whilst the mother is confined.

Although the majority of Gypsies do not marry in a church or registry office and their marriages are unrecorded, it is rare for a union among Romanies to break up. I have only known of one such case. On the few occasions when a marriage fails and the couple decide to part, the children are always cared for, either by one of the parents, usually the mother, or the grandparents, or some relative or friends. Homes for Gypsy orphans or the aged would have to close for lack of occupants. The Gypsies look after each other.

Serious crime and vice hardly exists among them. There are no Gypsy prostitutes – and no customers.

The Gypsies' enduring relationships and happy married life contrast very favourably with that other group of travellers, the mumpers, whose relationships are often feckless and temporary. A woman mumper, for instance, may have several children by different fathers, and rare indeed is it for the fathers to contribute anything towards their offspring's keep, or take an interest in their welfare once they have left the woman. Here one often meets with emotional unbalance in both children and adults. As far as his emotional and intuitive life is concerned the Gypsy is points ahead of many gorgios.

The Gypsy seldom reads a newspaper. Even more rarely does he read a book. Many travellers these days own portable wireless sets and enjoy listening to light music and singing. Events that throw the rest of the country into a turmoil – general elections, for instance – leave the Gypsy quite unmoved and uninterested. He never votes and it is all the same to him, or so he thinks, which party gets in. His energies, thoughts and emotions are directed solely to his own way of life.

The party of wagons split up in the late afternoon, three going to one farm and three to another. It was generous of the farmers to allow these travellers to put up in their fields for the night. Such hatchin-tans are not so easily come by.

The cranes were pushed into the ground, fires started, vegetables scrubbed, chopped, and placed in the cooking pots together with cuts of meat. Sliced carrot, turnip, potato, onions, parsley, wild thyme, sorrel, meat all went into the pots together to make a tasty and nourishing stew. After the meal was over and the utensils washed up, people relaxed.

I was to share a wagon which belonged to Lisha and her young husband, a Gypsy called Gilbert. He told me that he had been fined £8 already under the Vagrancy Act, not an inconsiderable sum for a Gypsy to have to pay. He and Lisha had been indicted by the police for such petty misdemeanours as camping on open ground a day longer than the Act decrees is allowable.

Tremendous pressure is being brought to bear on travellers by the police and local authorities these days. It is a constant cry of 'Move on, move on!' and continual efforts are being made to get the travellers off the roads and out of their wagons and into some sort of permanent dwelling. It is so much easier to keep track of people that way and, moreover, control them, from birth until death. There is nothing bureaucracy dislikes more than having its filing system out of order; a person's death registered but not his birth and so forth. And the bureaucrat is no doubt longing for the day, perhaps not so far off, when these last defaulters have been housed and docketed and are paying their

National Insurance and taxes regularly like the rest of us.

A considerable number of travellers do give up the life and 'settle down', not because they want to but because they are virtually compelled to do so. The threat of being told to move from a camping ground almost before the horses have been unharnessed, day after day and year after year, is sometimes more than the strongest nerves can stand. And so a couple may move into a small house and stay 'travellers' in name only.

Heavy rain started to come down while I was busy with my washing-up and I made for the wagon. Lisha's sister-in-law, Nell, came hurrying back from the farm with her two children sheltering under her coat. The girl had an arm round her mother's waist and the boy an arm round his sister's. The sight reminded me of a hen peewit holding a protective wing over its brood as she hurried them from some impending danger.

The rain stopped as suddenly as it had started. Lisha took a low canvas chair from the wagon and placed it outside. Then she set a pair of curling tongs on a small paraffin burner and called to her husband. Some male Gypsies take considerable pains over their appearance, while others let themselves go almost completely. It is quite a common practice for the men, particularly the younger ones, to have their hair tonged. Their mothers do it for them before they are married and after that their wives.

Gilbert sat himself down on the chair, a look of assumed boredom on his face.

'Get cracking quick,' he said. 'I want to go down to the pub with the others.'

He was a good looking youth of about twenty with dark brown hair. He sat relaxed and motionless, his hands submerged in the thick green grass. Although he sat so still, his whole lithe build gave an impression of swift and easy movement and powerful masculinity. It was this masculinity which made it possible for him to sit in the open field having his hair tonged. No passer-by scanning him over the hedge could have charged him with effeminacy.

Lisha did his hair in tight waves. 'Put your head this way,' she instructed.

Slowly he bent his head. His eyes were half closed and he smiled to himself as though he were reliving in memory some secret, happy event.

'Finished.' Lisha stood back to admire her handiwork. 'Pass the oil, please, Reena. It's on the bottom shelf of the cupboard, next the floor polish.'

I handed her the bottle of oil. She poured a goodly measure into her palm, then worked it into Gilbert's hair.

'That's fine,' she commented. 'Take a look at yourself.'

Waved, curlicued and glossed to perfection, he rose, yawned, and took a quick look at himself in the mirror she held before him, then he disappeared into the wagon. A few minutes later he reappeared again, having donned a cap and clean white scarf, the ends of which were tucked neatly under the revers of his jacket. He untied a whippet which was lying beneath the wagon, then he and two other men set off for the pub, the dog careering ahead of them.

'Don't forget to buy me a packet of crisps,' Lisha called out. She then turned to me, 'Now we're rid of them for a while. Will you read my duk?'

The Romanies are just as keen to have their palms read as gorgios if they think a person can really give a good dukkerin.

No sooner had Lisha and I sat ourselves down on the wagon steps than the other women and some children hurried over and I was confronted with a forest of outstretched hands. Lisha was annoyed.

'Leave off, can't you, till she's told mine! Oh, take your hands away – she hain't even started afore you all cut in.'

'Go on, tell hers quick, love, then tell mine,' said the great-great-grandmother with a hearty cackle. 'And I want you to tell the old man's too,' she added, 'when he gets back.'

Even the smallest children were eager to have their palms read and their mothers were not going to let me off the task. At one moment I found myself holding someone's fingertips and telling the fortune to another until I was duly corrected. The press of bodies was so great that it was not altogether easy to fit the hand to the owner. At last I had read the final palm and everyone appeared satisfied.

A brilliant sunset lit up the sky. Flaming orange and golden clouds were banked round the setting sun. Lisha and I, she carrying the baby, walked to a small pool at the far end of the field. Several aspen trees were growing by it. Lisha propped the baby up against a trunk and started to gather up some of last year's withered leaves. One by one, she placed the leaves on the water and blew them across the golden surface until the pond looked as though a swarm of curious insects had alighted on it.

The great orange sun was sinking behind the hills. Already one side of the pool had turned a deep black. Lisha continued to blow at a leaf which floated on the remaining gold. I sensed that her game would continue as long as the gold lasted. Now only a rim of sun showed above the hill. Lisha steered the leaf with a finger along the last thin strip of molten water. Then, without a flicker, the narrow strip of light went out as though some invisible person had leant over our shoulders and blown. The game was over. Lisha picked up the baby and we started back to the wagons. It was the brief, nameless period of the day when the sun has disappeared and no pale moon has yet arisen to take command of the heavens.

Late the following morning we left the farm. The day was cool with a grey sky across which scudded elongated clouds, like flocks of black swans. The rain held off. We travelled away from the main road through up-and-down country. The wind blew against us. The women and children sat in the carts talking among themselves; one held the reins and flicked a whip over the skewbald's rump. Lisha's hair streamed loose in the wind. A wagon rounded a bend of the road, standing out sharply from the sombre background. Not long after we had started, we met up with the rest of the travellers near the farm where they had pitched for the night.

The wagons travelled at a leisurely pace, up and down the hills like ships riding the waves. We passed a field of cabbages whose leaves creaked in the wind. We passed orchards and woodlands. As we climbed steadily upwards the countryside grew barer and the wind sang eerily through the telegraph wires.

Before the wagons and their owners split up and dispersed among three farms in the Honeybourne area, I left these Gypsies and continued on towards Stratford.

SEVEN

A Pitch Near the Avon

IF YOU TAKE A MAP of southern Britain and draw a line from Ludlow east through Bromsgrove to Warwick; from Warwick south to Shipston-on-Stour; from Shipston westwards to Tewkesbury, Ledbury and Hereford; and from Hereford northwards back to Ludlow, this rectangle encloses one of the most intensively cultivated areas in Britain, chiefly for fruit, hop, and vegetable growing. Except in rare instances, this cultivation has not spoilt the countryside but has added to its charm. The area consists of the most rural counties of England; a little of Shropshire, large areas of Herefordshire, Worcestershire and Warwickshire, and the northern tip of Gloucestershire. Northwards lies the big industrial town of Birmingham; south lie the Forest of Dean, the main Cotswold area and the water-meadow country of U-bend rivers and willow trees; eastwards lies the old town of Banbury; and westwards are the Black Mountains and Wales.

This region contains some of England's most beautiful towns and villages. Ludlow calls itself the most beautiful town in England, but there are others which, if not more beautiful, can equal it. Those pearls of the mid-west, for instance, Evesham in the heart of the fruit-growing country, and Ledbury, one of the main hopping towns. These two small towns, each with one main street and a weekly market, are centres of activity where country matters are concerned, and they attract to themselves and to the surrounding areas large numbers of travellers each season.

'If you can't pick your own – pick Smedley's!' runs the caption outside Smedley's canning factory in Evesham. During the three seasons I stayed in this fertile area, living as a Gypsy with Gypsies and earning my living like them, I certainly picked my own and a good many other people's – peas, beans, strawberries, raspberries, plums, tomatoes, apples, pears and hops.

Life hums as the picking season gets under way. Lorries and brake vans speed down the lanes and roads, filled with empty crates and piled high with sacks of produce, or stacked with fresh white chips – the small baskets in which are sold such soft fruit as strawberries and plums. Wagons and trailers move from farm to farm, wherever there is a need of pickers. One seems to be busy every moment of the day, for when the picking is finished there is the cooking, mending, laundry work, and hawking wares to be getting on with. It is a matter of pride for every travelling family to have some washing put on the line or spread over the bushes each day; even the mumpers pull their socks down during this season and put them into a pail for a wash every so often. A family or individual feels humiliated if the news gets around that they never seem to have any washing out.

It did not take me long to find the Boswells' wagon; a few questions at a pub and local Post Office and I soon located it in a field, with the two skewbalds grazing nearby. This was an old style wagon, horse-drawn, and painted in the traditional Romany colours of red, black and yellow. The door was closed.

'Mrs Kizer, are you there?' I called, climbing up the wooden steps and giving a rap. The travelling folk have a way of addressing the older married persons by the prefix Mr or Mrs, as the case may be, followed by the Christian name. Thus the two eldest members of this family were addressed as Mr Dan and Mrs Kizer, the surname Boswell being omitted.

Pitched alongside the wagon was a modern trailer belonging to Mrs Boswell's son Hiram. I heard footsteps inside the wagon and Mrs Boswell called, 'Come in, Reena.'

Mrs Kizer Boswell was a Welsh Gypsy. The Welsh Gypsies were the first Romanies I had got to know, and a very fascinating people I found them. Before her marriage she had been an Owen. She was Welsh, her husband was Welsh, and most of their numerous relatives were Welsh. During the winter months they usually pitched in a woodyard at the back of an isolated inn, and the men of the family made a living by selling logs and helping out occasionally at the inn and local farms. The women hawked. Mrs Kizer could dukker. She had three children: Hiram, a young man who was married, Deborah, the eldest daughter, who was also married, and Thurzie, the youngest daughter. Though the eldest children were married they still journeyed along with their parents, but in their own trailers. Thurzie shared her parents' caravan, or wagon. The married children and their families would travel on ahead of the old couple and Thurzie to the next hatchin-tan in their motor-drawn trailers.

Most of the Welsh Gypsies start travelling at the beginning of the picking season, in late spring or early summer. They hit a long drom (road). Apart from the London Gypsies, the Welsh are the greatest travellers. Whether they come from North or South Wales, the majority cross the border into Shropshire or the Marches and describe a rough circle during the spring, summer and autumn, before returning to Wales for the local horse fairs.

The first picking for which the farmer takes on a fair amount of hired labour is the pea crop. Then follow odds and ends for which he may or may not employ outside labour – lettuce, beans, new potatoes. The big crops, for the picking of which he employs the greatest number of travellers, are the plums and the hops. They are late summer and autumn crops. Every travelling family has its steady farms where it and its forbears have been taken on, sometimes for decades. The farmers like employing Gypsies. They are good workers and have their own roofs above their heads. They are no trouble as a rule. Tramps and mumpers he employs when there is no one else available. These people usually travel alone and are a feckless and undependable element. They call themselves travellers, but the Romanies call them trash. The farmer houses them in little shacks, rather like bathing huts, or in tents.

Mrs Kizer was alone when I went in. She seldom joined the other pickers now that she was elderly. Instead, she busied herself about the wagon and with the marketing and hawking. She told me that the rest of the family were only working half a day at this farm, picking beans. In the afternoons they walked down the road to help out at a market garden. There was a tan, or tent, erected not far from the wagon and trailer, and this I was to share with Thurzie – sleeping on a bed, I may say; the Gypsies never sleep on the ground. Our two beds were light truckle affairs, but quite comfortable.

Privacy does not exist in the Gypsy way of life, but I seldom find this oppressive with the country one step outside the door. Should the lack of privacy start irking me, then I can always say goodbye at short notice without giving offence. I never tell a Gypsy family that I wish to be on my own for a while, for a need for occasional periods of solitude which for many gorgios is something of a necessity – certainly in my own case – is one which the Gypsy simply does not understand. He or she is never alone except for the briefest periods, but the possibility that by some freak of circumstances he might be left stranded of human company is perhaps the Gypsy's greatest fear. In the old days the worst punishment that a Gypsy chief could inflict on a member of his clan was banishment from the tribe; a veritable fate worse than death, for no other tribe would accept the outlaw, and he would be forced to wander the roads alone until dying a miserable yet nevertheless welcome death under a tree or hedgerow like any low-down tramp.

It was still early in the day, and after I had drunk a cup of tea and unpacked my belongings I set off, at Mrs Kizer's request, for Stratford to buy some groceries and coloured crêpe paper at Woolworth's.

In the fields one works in gumboots turned over at the tops and one's most ancient clothes. But like most Gypsy women, I kept an old pair of court shoes for shopping and hawking expeditions. These I put on. Then I changed into a long-sleeved jersey, on top of which I wore a short-sleeved cotton blouse. An old linen skirt and a scarf around my head completed my attire. I arranged my shoulder-length hair in an elaborate style of plaits and ringlets, and fastened a pair of gold earrings to my ears.

'Shall I do a little hawking as well as the shopping?' I asked.

'Well, you can try and get rid of some of these ribbons and laces if you like,' said Mrs Kizer. 'But don't stay too long in town. I want to get on and make up a whole heap of flowers from the crêpe this evening.'

I filled the kipsie with lace and ribbons and, not forgetting my hawker's licence, set off.

The Stratford police are for ever asking the Gypsy women who sell their wares there for a look at their licences, and they are quick to 'book' anyone who has not got one. Too many travellers hawking their wares in the bard's birthplace may prove a nuisance to the visitors, so they think, and they do what they can to discourage it. Many of these visitors make excellent customers and their generosity compensates for any small inconvenience one may suffer from the attentions of the police. It is the foreign visitors who are especially generous and who usually seem pleased to meet a Gypsy hawking her wares and are willing to buy a strip of Olde English Lace recently purchased from Woolworth's or a paper or wood-shaving flower.

When I got off the bus I made straight for Woolworth's. Here I bought rolls of red, orange, yellow, pink, and light and dark green crêpe paper. Some thickish wire for stalks, fine wire for leaves and the tying on of petals, and a pot of glue. That is all the material needed to make paper flowers. I also bought bottles of scarlet and orange ink with which to dye the petals of the wood-shaving flowers that the men cut with their penknives. Sometimes cochineal is used instead.

Next I went to a bakery and bought a long loaf of bread, then into a fishmonger's for some kippers. Two large tins of baked beans completed my purchases. As I was walking idly along wondering whether to go straight back or try hawking the few wares I had with me, I felt a tap on my shoulder. On turning round I fully expected to see a figure in navy-blue who would demand to look at my licence. But instead it was a burly American with cameras and various photographic gadgets hung around his neck and over his shoulders.

'Have you got anything to sell?' he asked politely, though I was perfectly aware he was not interested in buying anything at all.

'Yes, plenty,' I said, delving into the kipsie. 'It's always nice to meet a visitor from America, Mister.'

'I'm from Canada,' he said, smiling.

'Oh, my mistake.' I never can tell the difference between the two accents. 'Is it something for yourself you'd like?' I asked, holding up some shoelaces, 'or for your wife?' And I produced some yards of white lace from the kipsie.

'Er, what I was really wondering,' he said uncertainly – and with all that photographic equipment it was not hard to guess what – 'was whether you'd be so kind as to let me take your photograph?'

I did not jump at the offer of being photographed; I brooded over it for several seconds. Sometimes having one's photo taken leads to hard cash while at others the camera enthusiast seems to expect you to pose for the sheer love of it.

'I should like to give you something – if you'll let me,' he said awkwardly. 'Very well, Mister,' I said after due deliberation, 'you may take my photograph. Where would you like me to stand?'

'Would you mind walking over to the square?'

We walked to the square and I posed with my kipsie over my arm while he took several snaps. Quite a little crowd started to gather round. Then he opened his wallet and took out a ten-shilling note.

'Oh, no, Mister – that's too much,' I said. There are limits to what one should accept on such occasions.

'Please, I should like you to have it,' he said.

He sounded so genuine that I finally accepted the note, thanked him, and we went our separate ways. I was still tucking the ten-shilling note safely into my pocket when a policeman swooped.

'The gentleman gave me the money, officer,' I said.

'I just want to have a look at your licence, please.'

He studied it carefully before handing it back. 'And now get moving. We don't like hawkers in Stratford.'

'I haven't hawked a thing,' I said. But there is no point in arguing with the law, one might as well save one's breath.

The fact is, a basketful of wares and a hawker's licence give one the right to knock on anyone's door, and one can hawk one's goods in town, village or country lane. So long as one does not make a nuisance of oneself and pester people to make purchases one is free to go where one wishes. No other trade gives one such a chance of taking a good look at all sorts of people, homes, and gardens, nor the chance of getting a glimpse into other people's lives. Many confidences are imparted to the Gypsy woman as she goes from house to house with her wares.

When I got back from my trip I found that everyone had returned from the fields. Our group comprised Dan and Mrs Kizer Boswell, their son Hiram, and his wife Fanny, and their two children, Lockwood and Eudocia. Thurzie and I brought the number to eight. Not far distant from 'our' field was Deborah, the Boswells' eldest daughter who was married to a man called Tarsh Hinde, and they had a baby called Chrissie. It did not take long to learn who had arrived in the vicinity, who had still to come, and on which farms and holdings the various families were working. Eudocia, a girl of about ten, was helping Thurzie prepare supper when I got back.

The first question I asked my tent-mate on seeing her again was whether she had made up her mind yet as to whom she was going to marry. For some years it had more or less been taken for granted that one day she would marry, or rommer, her cousin Euphryn whom she had known since she was a child. But the year before she had met a handsome young Gypsy called Isidor Fennet, to whom she had taken a great fancy, and he to her.

'Well, who's going to be the lucky man?' I asked.

Thurzie smiled. 'I still haven't decided for sure,' she said.

'But I will have by the end of the season – maybe sooner. I want to get rommerred this year and have my own trailer.'

Thurzie was a girl who was alert to every shade of emotion that rose and faded, and she could get behind the facade of words very easily and know whether people meant what they said or not and what they were really feeling, whatever sort of front they presented to the world. Her senses had developed and not slowly withered, as is the case with many people. She could be blunt and very direct in her speech at times, yet people seldom took offence.

During the day she did her hair in two short plaits, but for special occasions she would curl it and wear it loose. She and her brother Hiram had the same rather narrow, vivid faces, each marked with a certain mysterious quality which appealed to me. Both were inclined to occasional fits of moodiness and quick temper. The middle child, Deborah, was a plumper, more placid type and, though prettier, was not so attractive as her younger sister.

I helped slice some carrots. 'Where's Euphryn now, and where's Isidor?' I asked.

'Euphryn's down the road in the same field as Deb, and Isidor is way past the Trumpet.'

'My, that's a long way off.'

The Trumpet is a well known inn which stands at a crossroads on the Ledbury-Hereford road.

'They're only staying there a few days, then they'll be moving on to a farm near Harvington.'

'That's still a good way from here,' I said. 'It looks to me as though Euphryn has the better chance.'

'Which one's near and which one's far doesn't make any difference to me. I'm going to pick the one I love best.'

'Isidor wrote her ever such a nice letter,' said Eudocia. 'Are you going to show it to Reena?'

'Yes, she's welcome to read it if she'd care to.'

'I'll fetch it.'

'Isidor can read and write,' said Thurzie. 'I can't, and neither can Euphryn. It's no good pretending that being able to read and write doesn't help quite a bit these days. And there's another thing: Isidor and I aren't related and I think that's all to the good. He's told me that if we get rommerred we'll travel our own drom.'

Thurzie was very independent and I think she found it irksome at times being the only child left in her parents' wagon, and she was eager to set off and travel new roads.

Eudocia came running back holding a small piece of lined paper. Thurzie took it from her. 'Isidor sent word through one of our cousins that he was writing and that I was to fetch the letter from the Littleton Post Office,' she said.

'And who read it out to you?' I asked.

'I went to a pub and asked the barmaid to read it to me.'

'Read it out loud, Reena,' Eudocia requested.

They both sat down on their heels, chins cupped in their hands, while I read:

Darling Thurzie,

We should be up Harvington way at the same farm we worked first last year. And when we are there I am going to ask you again to rommer me. Believe me you had better say yes. I know that you are not going to rommer Ufrin whatever you say because you would have done it by now if you'd meant it, seeing as you've known each other 19 years.

There is nothing more I can say darling at this moment till we meet. And just to show you that I am quite series I am already looking out for a lorry and trailer.

You have all my love and kisses as always,

Goodbye, Sweeheart,

Isidor

'Well, what d'you think of it?' Thurzie asked. 'He certainly can write, can't he?'

'He certainly can,' I said. 'And I'll take a guess that you two will be rommerred before the season's out.'

'That's what I think,' said Eudocia. 'I hope I get a letter like that one day.'

Thurzie went to do some mending in the tan while Eudocia and I continued cooking supper in the heavy iron pot suspended over the yog. The year before I had taught her and Lockwood the Song of the Bird Scarers and I asked her whether she remembered it. In the old days, after the fields were ploughed, small children would walk up and down the furrows singing the song and shaking rattles.

'Yes, I remember it,' she said, and started to chant the song in her harsh voice:

> We've ploughed the land,
> We've sown the seed,
> We've made all neat and gay;
> So take a bit
> and leave a bit,
> Away, birds, away!

Lockwood came up then and asked if I had seen his new cage of linnets. Every wagon has a bird or two; usually three, four or more. I have seen finches, tits, budgies, canaries, tame blackbirds and thrushes, and once a pair of yellowhammers. Linnets are always popular because of their bright appearance and pleasant singing.

Lockwood unhooked the cage from the front of the trailer where the birds had been hung to get a breath of fresh air, and carried it over to the fire. There were six linnets inside the cage. Besides these birds, they also had a pair of canaries in another cage, while the old couple had a pair of green budgies which were often let out when the door and windows of the wagon were safely closed. The pair would perch on one's shoulder and accept crumbs from one's hand.

'Hark how they start chirping soon as I hang them back on the hook,' called Lockwood, who had been swinging the cage idly back and forth as he carried it to the trailer, causing the small occupants to flutter their wings in alarm.

That evening we ate together in the open as usual. No one went visiting or down to the pub as there was too much work that needed doing about the camp. I sat myself down on a stool by the yog and worked away making paper flowers until it got too dark to see what I was doing. Then I took the materials into the tan and continued working by the light of the paraffin lamp. I made pink and yellow roses, orange lilies, big scarlet peonies, and other flowers quite unknown to botanists. Thurzie was busy colouring the wood-shaving flowers which Hiram had whittled and dumped on the table. When a flower had been coloured she stuck it on a twig of everlasting greenery through the hole bored at one end. These wood-shaving flowers could sometimes be sold for as much as 1s. 6d. The paper ones usually sold for around sixpence each, a little less if the customer bought several. Frequently they would be bartered for such commodities as butter, eggs, fruit and vegetables. Bartering, or chopping, is done as much as selling and buying amongst travellers.

Fanny, Hiram's wife, came in presently, followed by the two children. She was a tall, deeply tanned young woman with aquiline features. When I looked at her I wondered whether the Romanies had in fact come from Egypt, as is supposed by some scholars, and not from India, as others think, for there was something very Egyptian about the cast of her face.

She asked me for the scissors I had been using to cut out petals and leaves, and sat herself down on my bed. 'What was that story you mentioned last year, Reena, about some gorgio chap being buried up in the Black Mountains – him with the Romany rovvel?'

The Romanies are avid for stories, particularly ones in which they figure, and adults will often come and listen with interest to a story which one is telling to the chavvies.

'Oh, tell us a story, Reena,' begged Eudocia. 'Don't have to be the one about the Romany rovvel and the gorgio chap if you don't remember it.

Anyone will do.'

'Shut up!' said Fanny. 'I want her to tell that one.'

'Goodness knows what that one was,' I said, collecting up the flowers and putting them into the kipsie. 'A gorgio chap buried somewhere in the Black Mountains who was married to a Romany rovvel. . .'

'Yes, he died somewhere in the Black Mountains and she went off to look for a special kind of leaf that would bring him back to life again.'

'Ah, yes, now I remember. That's the story of Chaya and Lynndon,' and I started to tell it to them again.

This story of a pair of ill-starred lovers, Chaya the Gypsy girl, daughter of a shevengro or Gypsy chief, and Lynndon, son of a wealthy borro rye, ends with the pair wandering in the Black Mountains, having flung off their pursuers, irate members of the Gypsy tribe who are incensed at one of their members having married a gorgio. But they escape them only to be parted by death for Lynndon succumbs to the cold. In an agony of grief, Chaya sobs over her dead husband, and as she does so the snow starts falling from a grey sky. The flakes remind her of swan feathers. A swan feather used to be a token of love between Gypsies, and she had given one to Lynndon as an assurance of her love for him. Kneeling beside him, she sings:

> Come slowly down, slowly swan feathers,
> From the grey skies above,
> And weave a white mantle
> To cover my love.
>
> Freeze, freeze the white mantle
> East wind with your breath,
> And guard him, dark pines,
> As he slumbers in death.
>
> Now I'll wander, I'll wander
> The earth till I see
> The silver and green
> Of the Eildon Tree.

The Eildon Tree is the tree of magic and it was once believed that if a lover should lose the beloved one through death and the tree could be found, then a leaf plucked from its branches and laid on the breast of the dead one would restore him or her to life again and the pair be reunited.

It is said that Chaya is still searching for the Eildon Tree and that Lynndon still sleeps in his ice coffin high up in the Black Mountains, as beautiful as on the day he died. Only when the Romanies unite with the gorgios and the wild is mingled with the tame will Chaya find the tree, so it is said. Then she will pluck a leaf and return with it to Wales and lay it on Lynndon's breast.

'And that time can't be far off,' I ended, 'because these days the Romanies and gorgios are intermarrying as never before.'

'That's true,' said Fanny. 'There's more diddikais than Romanies now. In a few years' time, I reckon, there won't be any pure-bred Romanies left.'

She and the children said goodnight and went to their trailer.

As the breeze blew in through the open flap of the tent, I wondered if I would ever be able to sleep contentedly in a house again, cut off from close proximity with earth, grass and wind by a barrier of bricks and mortar.

EIGHT

In the Fields and Elsewhere

DURING THE SEASON the families work as a single unit and get paid for what they pick. I worked with the Boswells, and I asked Hiram, who collected the pay, to give me thirty shillings a week; the rest of my earnings, which probably amounted to around £7, were to go into the common pool. I did not pay them for the use of the tent or for food. Anything I earned hawking I split in two and handed over one half, for the families to use as they thought best. This arrangement suited them and myself; there was never any quibbling over money matters whilst I was with them.

The pea season was now in full swing and we worked a full day in the fields. Thurzie and I would work along a row together, seldom speaking as we pulled the pods from the stalks. She picked quicker than I did and never seemed to tire. Although my back ached less than it had done at the start of the season, I was still finding a full day's work something of a strain; 'back breaking' is a very apt phrase where pea-picking is concerned. Sometimes I picked standing, bent over double. Then, to vary my stance and relieve my aching muscles a little, I would kneel down on a sack and work my way along the row on my knees. This position, too, grew very wearing after a while. Hiram and Fanny would work a nearby row together, and the children and Dan Boswell another. We kept together as a group and mixed little with the local field hands, though there was no unfriendliness.

Sometimes old Dan Boswell and the children would quit work at midday. Being able to take time off is one of the good things about this life for older people who have families. They can put in a full day, a few hours, or stay away altogether for a day should they not feel like working. The farmer expects, of course, that the bulk of his hired labour will put in a full day during busy periods. If a family proves slack, then they do not get taken on again the following year. The Boswells had worked at this farm for three generations, and the farmer told me that he preferred Gypsies to any other workers, even the local hands, as they worked harder and never grumbled if he should ask them to put in extra hours in the evenings should a crop have to be harvested quickly.

We did not go back to the wagon for lunch, but had a good hearty snack and several flasks of tea in the field by the hedgerow. Often Euphryn, Thurzie's cousin and suitor, would bicycle over from a nearby field and we would discuss plans for the evening: whether he should come up to our field, whether we should go down to his, or whether to go to the pub for glasses of beer and cider and a game of darts.

As each day passed Thurzie seemed less set on him as a possible husband and more keen on the still-absent Isidor. She was constantly begging me to take over Euphryn when Isidor arrived in the vicinity, so that she would be free to have him to herself without Euphryn hanging around.

'I'm sorry, but Euphryn's not my type,' I informed her. He was a fair, solidly built Gypsy, and although pleasant in manner, he lacked vitality and emotional sensitivity, and I found him somewhat boring.

'He grows on you,' Thurzie assured me. 'He's not a man you get to know quickly.'

'Well, he doesn't seem to be growing on you,' I said. 'Every day you talk more and more about Isidor.'

One evening as we were sitting round the yog after supper, with Euphryn alongside Thurzie, there was a loud joter (Romany hail), and there was Isidor climbing over the gate with another Gypsy.

They were both about the same height, tall and well built, and they laughed and talked together as they walked towards us. As I watched them approaching, the feeling grew within me, until it became a certainty, that this other Gypsy, whoever he might be, would come to mean something to me and that because of him my life would undergo a change, and that I would be instrumental in changing his.

Isidor, after greeting us, sat himself down on the other side of Thurzie, and the stranger came and sat beside me. He gave me a brief look before starting a conversation with Dan Boswell and I wondered whether his feelings had been akin to my own.

'This is Jai,' Isidor informed the company. 'His trailer's hatched alongside ours.'

Two more mugs were filled with tea.

'In another day our field will be stripped,' said Isidor, 'but we're stopping on at the same farm. In a short while there'll be the strawberries to pick.'

'That's my favourite crop,' said Thurzie.

'Yes, because you enjoy eating them. But hops is more fun,' said Hiram. 'There's always a good crowd in the hop fields. Have you got some days off coming?'

'I reckon we'll have about four,' Isidor said. 'I've got plenty to be getting on with. I want to touch up the vardo among other things and go out and have a look at one or two trailers and lorries I've heard about.'

'Oh, so you're thinking of buying a trailer,' commented Hiram.

'Yes. I'm keeping my eyes open for a good second-hand one. There's usually plenty for sale around this way.'

Euphryn's expression had become forbidding and I was afraid there might be a scene.

'What's this trailer for – you thinking of getting rommerred or something?' Hiram asked. He always enjoyed putting a match to dry tinder.

'Yes, as a matter of fact, I am,' said Isidor.

'That's interesting news,' said Dan Boswell with a smile. 'I hope we'll be asked to the rommerin supper.'

'You can rely on that. And now, may I ask Thurzie down to the pub for a glass of cider?'

'She happens to be going down with me,' cut in Euphryn.

'Well, in that case, let's all go down together,' said Isidor amiably and with an assurance that must have troubled his contestant somewhat. 'Who's that young lady sitting next to Jai maybe she'd like to come along too?'

'That's Reena,' said Thurzie. 'She's staying along with us for the season. You're coming down for a drink, aren't you, Reena?'

'Yes, I should like to come,' I said.

'Good, that makes a fair crowd,' said Isidor.

Thurzie, Euphryn and Isidor walked on ahead, but before the rest of us started after them Dan Boswell said to his son, 'I'm asking you to see to it that they don't get fighting.'

'I'll keep them apart,' said Hiram.

'Mind you do. Keep the party pleasant.'

We drove down to the pub in Jai's small brake van which was parked outside the gate. Again that curious feeling came over me that this man would in some way affect my life. I regarded him closely from the back seat, wondering what sort of a person he was. During the time we had been sitting round the fire he had hardly said a word.

The pub was crowded with locals and travellers, and it was difficult to find a seat, so we stood in a line against the wall, Thurzie between her two contenders and I between Jai and Hiram. Fanny had stayed behind to mind the children.

This pub was unlike many, in that travellers were welcome. Sometimes in the picking areas of Wales, and other parts of Britain which are frequented by travellers, I have seen notices in the pubs: 'No Gypsies served here' or, more briefly, 'No Gypsies'. What an outcry there would be, and rightly too, if the pubs displayed notices reading: 'No Negroes'. But as it is, these notices rarely excite comment from local people, from the clergy or council members, and no one writes letters to the press about them. Yet Gypsies surely have their claims too. They have been natives of these islands for centuries and, contrary to popular opinion, have worked hard, have inspired many artists, and have committed few of the major crimes of mankind. Are they not entitled to service without discrimination in our pubs? Gypsies were amongst the millions murdered in the terrible German concentration camps during the last war not so many years ago. No memorial stands to them.

I sipped my cider slowly. Not a few feet away a game of darts was in progress. The darts winged their way to the board along a dangerously narrow space, missing the backs of heads, eyes and noses by the merest inches. But nobody seemed to worry. Isidor placed his empty mug on the counter, and on returning he asked me in a low voice whether I would do something for him – write a letter to Thurzie which I was to give her on our return to the tan.

'I can write a bit,' he said, 'but I don't doubt that you can write better. Let's go outside for a few minutes.'

As we left the crowded bar Euphryn's momentary look of relief changed to one of deep suspicion.

Isidor and I seated ourselves at a small iron, green-painted table in a little garden. He took a wad of lined paper and a pencil from his pocket, together with an envelope, and handed them to me.

'What I'd like you to say is this,' he began, his eyes fixed on the table. 'Tell her I love her and want to rommer her and she's to give me her answer, whether she'll agree to be my rovvel, two evenings from now. Say I'll wait for her by the gate close by that big elm we passed on the way along. I know she's fond of me and I want to close the deal quick. Don't give her the letter till you're alone together. Let her open the envelope and then read out the letter to her.' He turned to me and smiled. 'It's best to get rommerred early in the season; the winter can be tough on newly-weds. Please write the letter in your own words.'

'Very well.'

I picked up the pencil. This was not the first time I had been asked to write a letter for a traveller concerning an affair of the heart. I made the letter brief and couched it in language which I hoped would appeal to Thurzie and make her accept Isidor's proposal. To me, he seemed a far more attractive and suitable partner for her than the stolid Euphryn. When I had finished I read it out and Isidor appeared well satisfied with what I had written.

'That's fine,' he said.

He folded the letter and slipped it into the envelope, wrote 'Thurzie' on the front, then handed it back to me.

'Have you a pocket where it'll be safe?'

'Yes, I'll put it in my skirt pocket,' I said.

Just then Jai came out. He drew up a chair and seated himself at the table. 'Finished the letter writing?' he enquired of me.

I nodded.

'Well, then, I've got something to ask you – what are you doing this coming Saturday?'

'I haven't planned to do anything,' I replied.

'Then come over to the farm where I'm pitched and have a cup of mookerimungeri in my trailer. I'll come and pick you up in the brake.'

I looked out at the darkened garden and felt the warm night air on my face. For a second I paused before answering. That brief pause, as I realised later, was the last moment in which my life continued one way; after it my life turned in another direction.

'Thank you,' I said. 'I should like to come.'

'Good. I'll fetch you around midday.'

'He's pure-bred Romany,' said Isidor, laughing. 'Think yourself lucky he's asked you to visit him.'

'No, only half,' said Jai, then asked me, 'Can you rokker Romany?'

'I'm afraid not. I've picked up a few words here and there; a few words of Welsh, too, and a few words of Cant.'

'Is it the Welsh travellers you know?'

'Yes, most of the travellers I know are of Welsh extraction. You're Welsh, aren't you?'

'Half of me, anyway.'

'You shouldn't do things by halves, Jai,' said Isidor, 'it's bad policy.'

'You don't have much choice in matters of that sort.'

Isidor stubbed the butt of his cigarette in an ashtray and we went back to the crowded bar. Standing in exactly the same place as we had left them were Thurzie, Hiram and Euphryn. They looked as though they had not said a single word to each other. Isidor signalled to them over the heads of the crowd. 'We've got to get going,' he called.

Thurzie looked at me intently, seeming to be satisfied at what she saw in my face. We walked out into the yard where the brake was parked. Euphryn was dropped first, then Thurzie, Hiram and myself. We talked for a while by the gate before the two drove off.

'Well?' Thurzie asked at once when we had entered the tan and lit the lamp.

I took the letter from my pocket and handed it to her. 'Open it,' I said.

She looked at me and, taking the letter out of the envelope, studied the writing intently. 'You wrote it, didn't you?'

'Yes,' I answered. 'Isidor asked me to. Give it back and I'll read it out.'

She sat down on the bed. On her face was a half smile not unlike the one I had seen on the youthful Gilbert's when he was having his hair tonged. As I read out the words I had written only a short while back they sounded new and strange to me. When I had finished reading, Thurzie said, 'I've made up my mind now; I'll rommer Isidor. He's the one I love best. Poor old Euphryn. I hope he doesn't take things too bad. That was a beautiful letter, Reena.' She stared up into the pointed roof into which the lamplight barely penetrated. 'It's strange to think that soon I'll be travelling along with a husband. One day you're living with your parents' vardo, and the next you're with the man you've chosen, travelling the drom with him. I've always been happy enough, yet as long as I can remember I've been looking forward to being a woman and leading my own life with my husband. Being grown up is a thousand times better than being a child. I reckon that it's only people who can't take life who're always harking back to the days when they were chavvies and saying they'd like to return to their early years again. D'you agree?'

'Yes. I've no wish to go back to the days when I was a child. Life's a case of going forward, moving on with no regrets.'

She regarded me thoughtfully. 'Have you ever thought of settling?'

'That's an odd question for a Gypsy to ask,' I said.

'I mean, have you never thought of travelling along with a man?'

'No,' I said, 'never.'

The goal which the majority of women set their hearts on had not been my goal, and the very thought of settling down for life in a house along with a husband was enough to bring on an acute attack of claustrophobia.

'I wonder. . . ?' Thurzie said.

I did not ask her what she was wondering about, and a silence fell between us. She lay stretched out on the bed, the light shining on her thick waved hair which she had unplaited. Tall and strong, like the rest of her family, she had told me once that she had only had a single bout of retching during her life, the only sickness which had kept her in the wagon for a few days. Other than that, she had never been ill.

'I'll keep his letter under my pillow tonight,' she said. 'There's no harm in being sentimental once in a while. Maybe next year I'll be a mother. But Isidor will always come first with me before any chavvy. No Romany woman puts her children before her man, unless he happens to be a low-down.'

'That's how it should be,' I said. 'Some gorgio women marry –'

We both turned at the same moment and looked towards the opened doorway. A figure, holding a lighted cigarette in one hand, stood there.

When he spoke, my blood, to use a well-worn phrase, ran very cold indeed.

'Poor old Euphryn!' he grated. 'I hope he doesn't take things too bad. Not half, you don't.'

'How long have you been listening outside, you beng!' shouted Thurzie.

'When the others dropped me off I picked up my bike and came down here. I heard what you were talking about together.'

Euphryn came in and sat himself on Thurzie's bed. 'I wanted to hear that letter read out. I guessed that Isidor had given Reena one. Well, it's been interesting all right.'

'I'm glad you enjoyed yourself,' said Thurzie. 'And now that you know what I feel like about Isidor, you can clear out of the tan.'

'I'm not getting out just yet. Before we start on the subject of you and Isidor, there's something else I want to say first. Reena's going to clear out and clear off. I knew all along she's been putting you against me. It's a pity Aunt Kizer ever let her stay with you. Anyway,' he continued, his voice dangerously low, 'take a hint from me, Reena. Pack your things tomorrow and hit the drom. The further you get from here the healthier you'll find it.'

'Oh, shut up, Euphryn!' said Thurzie. 'D'you think I can't make up my own mind and that I need Reena to do it for me? She's never said a word against you. And now I'll tell you something that'll make you laugh. Only a short while back I told Reena that I was more set on Isidor than on you, and what a good thing it would be if you and she could take a fancy to each other!' And Thurzie let out a peal of laughter.

Euphryn looked as though he was about to strangle her and then as though he would like to strangle me first.

'You shut up!' he bellowed. 'Stop laughing, or I'll pull you from the tan and chuck you into the ditch outside.'

'You'll be first in if you try that,' said Thurzie.

Having heard the raised voices, Hiram and Fanny appeared at the doorway.

'Has Euphryn been proposing?' Hiram asked his sister.

Thurzie continued to laugh, but I could not see that the situation was so amusing and I felt a deep sense of relief when Hiram and Fanny had put in an appearance. Hiram turned to his cousin and asked, 'What are you doing here at this time of night? You know there'll be the hell of a row if Dad finds out.'

'I'll tell you what he was doing,' said Thurzie. 'He was listening outside the tan while Reena read out a letter to me from Isidor. And he went on listening a good while after that.'

Euphryn clenched his fists and looked as though he were about to commence a tirade, but before he got going Hiram said mildly, 'You'd better be moving off down the road, Euphryn. It's late.'

Without a word, Euphryn left the tent. After a minute or so had gone by, Fanny said, 'Well, goodnight. Maybe we can get some sleep now.'

Silence spread quickly over the small encampment. Thurzie removed her outer garments and got into bed. I changed into a pair of cotton pyjamas, turned out the lamp, and did likewise.

My practice of changing into night attire was considered odd, almost indecent, by Thurzie. The Gypsies, who are acquainted with all the facts of life from early childhood and have in many cases witnessed, birth, copulation and death before they enter their teens, are nevertheless often shocked by nakedness. This is because they seldom see a naked figure. People usually wash in pieces, perhaps the top half one evening and the bottom half the next; the whole body is seldom exposed to view, which had been the case at first when I removed pants and petticoat before getting into my pyjamas.

'Dordi!' Thurzie exclaimed. 'I'd never do that in a thousand years.'

'Don't look so shocked,' I said. 'We're both girls, aren't we?'

'Very well,' she replied slowly. 'Please be careful never to have all your clothes off when Ma's around. She'd get the shock of her life, for sure.'

This attitude of Thurzie's had amused me. Needless to say, Mrs Kizer and the rest had soon got to hear of this practice of mine of stripping my clothes off each night and changing into pyjamas, and Mrs Kizer had informed me, somewhat sternly, that although she had been married at sixteen and she was now sixty-six, or thereabouts, she had never yet seen her husband without any clothes. 'And what's more,' she had added, 'I don't want to!'

That night I woke with a start when one of the big dogs, which were let loose at dusk, came running into the tent, snuffled under my bed, then ran out again. His pal, another half-breed monster, was sitting outside. Thanks to these guardians, who did their jobs well, we were never troubled in the encampment by mischievous persons during the day or at night.

We woke to the sound of heavy rain falling. From the opening of the tent, I saw Hiram run from the trailer to a nearby elm to get the fire going. They had a stove in their trailer, which was very useful for early morning cooking, and most mornings we all boiled our kettles on it, but Fanny had forgotten to exchange the bottled gas cylinder for a fresh one and the gas had run out. So on this wet morning it was a case of someone having to get the fire going.

Hiram left his family's kippers in a frying pan on the tripod and the next time I glanced out black smoke was belching from the pan.

'Your kippers!' I shouted.

Fanny's head appeared at the window of the trailer, and the next moment Lockwood darted from the doorway and ran towards the fire.

'Dordi!' he cried. 'They're all black and stuck to the bottom.'

'Of course they are,' said Thurzie. 'One of you should have been watching them. Get the kettle boiled and some tea made. It's too wet to bother with cooking.'

The rain came down harder than ever. So far the tent had proved weather-worthy, but every minute the ground outside was becoming more of a morass and slow rivulets of water were beginning to seep under the canvas. I kicked off my shoes and pulled on my gumboots. Through the falling sheet of grey water I saw Mrs Kizer beckoning me over to the vardo. I flung my mackintosh over my head and ran out into the downpour.

'I thought you'd like to take a look at my jewellery, seeing as it's so wet that you won't be working this morning,' she said. 'I never chop these pieces. Most of them have been in the family for years. This piece here Dan gave me when we were rommerred.'

I picked up a heavy gold brooch and admired it. It was formed in a circle, the outer edge plaited, whilst in the centre were entwined the initials D and K. Rings, earrings, bracelets and necklaces were spread out before me. This collection must have been worth quite a small fortune. Some of the rings were set with jewels; diamonds, rubies, topaz and amethyst. In a gold heart fastened to a chain was a strand of hair cut from the head of Leah Kalvi, the young wife of a Gypsy shevengro, who had died in her late twenties in the last decade of the nineteenth century. She had been distantly related to the Boswells. Gypsy shevengros, so Mrs Kizer informed me, exist to this day, but they do not hold the power they once did. Before the outbreak of the First World War their power was very considerable. In those days, as in these, the gorgios had little idea as to whom these chiefs and their wives might be. Only when one died and the Gypsies gathered from different parts of the country to attend the funeral did the non-Gypsy world become aware that a Romany notable had died and that the tribal members and friends had come to pay their last respects. In those days, whenever a Gypsy died all his belongings, jewellery excepted, were destroyed by burning. Everything was put into the wagon and this was set alight. If the Gypsy was buried in a churchyard, paper flowers and candles were set on the grave after the funeral ceremony, but it was not often that a headstone was erected. The Gypsies who were not buried in a graveyard were usually buried secretly in woodlands, and this still happens on occasions when it is known that the deceased's birth and marriage had never been registered. Unknown to the authorities and the rest of the outside world he or she has passed through life, and the only persons to know and mourn the passing at the secret graveside will be a small crowd of fellow travellers.

'It's a beautiful collection of jewellery, Mrs Kizer,' I said.

'I'm proud of it. This bracelet here and this brooch I'm giving to

Thurzie when she gets rommerred. I must say I'm glad she seems to have almost made up her mind, even though the young man isn't to be Euphryn.'

'Yes,' said Mr Dan, 'it's about time she made up her mind. I don't believe in a girl being unmarried after eighteen or thereabouts or a man after twenty-two. Past that age they start getting too pernickety and choosy. Euphryn's around twenty-four now and that's too late, by my reckoning, for getting rommerred.'

'How old were you when you got rommerred, Mr Dan?' I asked.

'I must have been about nineteen.'

He got up and pulled a medium-sized leather trunk from under the bed. The bed in the old-type wagon is built across the back; just under the rear window.

'I'll show you the jacket I wore on the day I was rommerred,' he said. 'These jackets were worn on special occasions right up to the time of the First World War. And the women wore shawls over their shoulders, and skirts down to the ankles which were made from some flowered material – they wore several skirts, more often than not, one on top of the other, so they swung out as they walked, and looked very pretty. Sometimes they wore a coloured apron over the skirt.'

From the trunk he took out a brown velvet jacket, down the front of which was a row of silver buttons.

'I wore a pair o' corduroy breeches which came to my knees,' he continued, 'rather like what them shooting and sporting ryes call. . .'

'Plus-fours?' I enquired.

'That's right. And a pair of high leather chokkers. I fancied myself to be very smart when I was a young man dressed like that.'

'Were these buttons made from silver coins?'

'Yes. The coins were hammered smooth and then shaped into buttons. Sometimes golden sovereigns would be made into buttons.'

These 'best' costumes of the Romanies remained almost unchanged up to the Great War and were being worn in George Borrow's day. The women wore coin necklaces of silver coins interspersed with a few gold sovereigns should the family be wealthy. Velvet and corduroy were much fancied. And the Romany tongue was really a secret language. Nowadays the younger persons hardly trouble to learn it and in one more generation, I believe, it will be a 'dead' language.

'Before the First War no Gypsy went into a hospital,' said Mrs Kizer. 'We had our own cures, and very good most of them were. I still use many of them myself, but the young ones prefer made-up medicines from the chemist. There's nothing like dock leaves and sorrel for clearing the blood, nor a pick-me-up than elder-flower tea.'

'Yes,' I agreed, for I had sampled some of these tonics and remedies. 'And wild herbs go well, too, in salads and soups. It's surprising how much free food goes untouched by the gorgio.'

'It is, dear. Tell me, what leaves do you put in salads? I'm not partial to salads myself.'

'Well, I put in young dandelion leaves to give a sharper taste, sometimes sorrel for a change, and samphire and salad burnet. Wild watercress I put in soup because as a gorgio I'm afraid of getting fluke if I eat it raw.'

'Fluke and all internal worms can be cured by a brew made from the bark and leaves of the elder, or, better still, from the roots of the male fern. And now, seeing as it's still raining, we'll have a cup of mookerimungeri.'

She poured the tea from a silver teapot into three pretty cups decorated with gold rims and coloured flowers.

'Do you reckon, Mr Dan,' I asked, sipping my tea, 'that the Romany life was more fun in your young days than it is now?'

'What a question to ask him,' said Mrs Kizer. 'Don't young men always have more fun than the older ones?'

Mr Dan laughed. 'I certainly had fun in my young days, but I'm still enjoying life.'

'What I really meant was, was the Romany life as a whole more enjoyable, say, before the First War, than it is in these days?'

'It was ever so much better in my younger days than it is now. For one thing, a lot of Romanies still travel like we do by horse-drawn wagon, and these days the roads are made for motor traffic. That makes travelling difficult, as you know.

'It was ever such a fine sight in the old days to see the gigs, and carriages, and traps. And there were all sorts of horses on the roads the likes of which you hardly ever see now; great strong drays for the heavy carts with puffs of hair round the hooves, trotters for the light gigs, and us Romanies used to keep one skewbald for the open traps. Very useful for getting to a place quick – and getting away quick, maybe. A traveller in those days could make a good living by just trading horses. And there were so many horse shows and fairs it was hard to make your mind up which ones to go to and which to miss. I remember one week in Plynlimon trading six gries (horses) and making a clear £150, and that was money in those days. Romany life has never been for lliprynnod (weaklings), but in the old days it was more free and easy somehow, if you were strong and healthy, in spite of the gavvers. They was around as usual, of course.

'But I'll tell you one thing to the good about these days: there aren't half so many tramps and mumpers on the drom. A regular nuisance they used to be, and half the time we'd get the blame for their thieving ways. If the last of them was cleared off the drom tomorrow I'd go up to the first gavver I met, shake him by the hand, and say, Good work, officer!'

I sat chatting with the old couple for the rest of the morning. Hiram and Fanny had taken the car into Stratford and exchanged the empty gas cylinder for a new one, and an appetising lunch was being cooked up on their stove. That was another point in favour of modern Gypsy life, I thought: gas stoves, not to mention cars which could be speeded into the nearest town and a fresh cylinder collected, thus doing away with the unpleasant necessity of cooking over a smoky fire under a tree whose leaves did not offer adequate shelter from a downpour.

The old days as extolled by Mr Dan certainly had their advantages, but there was a lot to be said in favour of Romany life today.

NINE

An Invitation

T HAT SAME AFTERNOON I set off by bicycle through a heavy drizzle on a mission for Thurzie. I went to a farm near Harvington with a letter from her, written by myself, which I was to deliver to Isidor. It was to inform him that Euphryn had overheard me when I was reading out his letter to Thurzie, and not to come over on the evening he had stated, and that Thurzie accepted his offer of marriage and would he come over on Saturday morning instead to discuss things.

Isidor was living in a tan next to his parents' wagon, and when I arrived on the scene he was sitting in the wagon reading a story out to them from a paperback. I delivered my missive, and was asked to sit down for a cup of tea.

The kettle is kept permanently on the simmer on wet days when the family is not working, and sometimes on such a day I have lost count of the cups of tea I have drunk.

'Good news or bad?' asked Isidor, ripping open the envelope.

'Good news,' I replied.

He smiled broadly.

'It was kind of you to come over all this way in the rain, lady,' said his mother.

'Call her Reena, mother,' said Isidor.

'I'll call the young lady whatever she likes to be called.'

'Please call me Reena,' I said. 'That is the name my travelling friends know me by.'

'And a nice name too, I must say.' Mrs Fennet wore her hair coiled over her ears. She had a lean, intelligent face. Her husband was a broad-backed jovial Gypsy who was wearing a red neckerchief.

'Here comes a nosey-parker,' he remarked, as there came the sounds of slow footsteps swishing through the grasses. A figure appeared at the upper half of the doorway; an old granny with a china bowl in one hand who did not so much as glance at Isidor who was reading the letter.

'I was just wondering if you could spare one or two lumps of sugar, love?' she said to Mrs Fennet. 'Or a couple of teaspoons of granulated would do as well – it's all the same to me.'

'Take what you want Sarah,' said Mrs Fennet, passing her the bowl from the table.

'Thanks. Just a couple of lumps for a cup will be plenty,' she said, helping herself to a handful. 'What you reading there, Isidor,' she enquired casually – 'somebody sent you a letter?' and she opened the door and shuffled in.

'That's right.'

'From Thurzie, I reckon. Did this young lady bring it over?'

'Yes, she did.'

'That was good of her now, very kind, specially in this weather.'

'I'm much obliged to her.'

'Well, what's the news from Thurzie – is she going to take you on?'

Isidor smiled but said nothing to this question.

'Don't keep me standing here all day, Isidor!' snapped the old crone.

'Can't a man keep any secrets to himself, Sarah?' asked Mr Fennet.

'Not if I can help it. It don't do men no good to hug secrets to themselves; that's what I've always said. How about you, Sophie?'

'I guess it's not good for a man to have too many,' replied Mrs Fennet.

'Too many! My old man don't have one, never did since he rommerred me, and he's been all the better for it. If there's any secrets to be kept, I'm the one who keeps 'em. Remember that, Isidor. Don't have any secrets from your wife. If she's smart she won't let you, anyway. My, he's looking pleased with himself, ain't he, Sophie? It don't strike me that Thurzie's turned him down.'

Her eyes, remarkably alert ones, switched to me. 'And so you're the young lady who's come over special with that letter?'

'Yes, that's right.'

'And will you be staying along with the Boswells for the season?'

'I reckon so.'

'You can never reckon for sure on anything in this world, dear. Time you found that out by now.'

'True enough,' I said.

I thanked Mrs Fennet for the tea, walked down the steps behind the old woman and took hold of the bike. As I wheeled it over the soggy ground she walked beside me and laid a restraining hand on my shoulder.

'I got a message for you, dear – part of the reason why I came over. It's from the young man in that trailer over there. He used to be pitched next to the Fennets, but this morning he took himself off over there by himself.' She pointed to a cream-coloured trailer parked close by the hedge a little apart from the others. 'The vardo nearest to his trailer is ours,' she went on. 'We painted it up before we started off this season, or rather, my old man did. This young man says he'd like a word with you before you leave. You know who I'm talking about, don't you? Jai. Soon as he saw you come he asked me to go across to the Fennets. I happened to be going anyway. Blast me! I've been and forgotten my sugar bowl. Well, I'll leave it there for a while. It'll give me a good excuse to go over again later and find out whether Isidor's going to get rommerred early or late this season. He and Thurzie will make a fine couple.'

As I walked towards the trailer the door opened and Jai came out. I pushed the bike through the crowd of children who asked if they might ride it round the field and down the lane.

'You can ride it down the lane, but not out on to the road,' I said. 'And you're not to keep it for long.'

'Come in and welcome,' said Jai.

I walked up the steps and into the modern trailer. Jai closed the door and we sat down on a bunk. He was dressed in corduroy trousers and a navy-blue sweater with a jacket on top. Round his throat he had twisted a scarf.

'What's the news?' he asked. 'Have you been acting as carrier pigeon for Thurzie?'

'That just about describes it. Euphryn happened to eavesdrop while I was reading out a letter to Thurzie from our friend across the field,' and I related the events of the previous evening.

He listened intently, yet without curiosity, sometimes turning his head away to glance out of the window. His short brown hair was waved and the eyebrows and lashes were several shades darker than the hair itself. His face, which was well fleshed and tanned, was somewhat long with high cheekbones. It was an open face which held a certain reserve; a face which did not lack mystery. His best feature were his eyes – as is often the case with someone who lives most of their life in the open. Large, clear, and alert, with the pupils coloured a dark amber. As he listened to me or talked in his turn, he would stretch out an arm to adjust a curtain or swing one of his long legs over the other. Every gesture, as well as his moments of repose, proclaimed a healthy body.

'I don't think that Euphryn's going to make things very pleasant for you from now on,' he said. 'He strikes me as being one of them people who easily gets a down on others for no particular reason. Why don't you clear off and come over here?'

'Well, that wouldn't be so easy,' I said. 'I've got no wagon, no roof over my head, and farmers aren't so keen on hiring a single woman.'

'Yes, that's true.' He leant back and folded his arms under his head.

The way he spoke this simple phrase seemed to turn it into a question. He smiled at me but said nothing more.

A silence grew, broken only by the swish of rain on the wagon roof and the panes, but it seemed to form a bridge between us and not an abyss of separation which is often the case when two strangers meet and the conversation dies.

The view from the window was obscured by a fresh downpour. I looked about the trailer. It was well kept. In one corner was a triangular walnut chest with glass panels in front, the kind which is often found in the old-type vardos. This chest was filled with a flowered tea set, and on the top shelf was a heavy silver teapot and jug. 'Romany,' I said to myself.

He was watching me closely. 'My mother was a Romany,' he said.

His words gave me a start, and I wondered for a moment whether he had read my thoughts.

'Would you like to take a look round the trailer?' he asked.

'Yes, please,' I said eagerly. Wagons and trailers of different kinds interest me greatly and I never tire of looking them over.

In this trailer, apart from the spacious living room, there was a kitchen with sliding doors and a separate toilet and wash basin. There was a modern gas stove. But outside the trailer I had noticed a smoking fire and a crane, and I guess he did little cooking on the stove except, perhaps, morning breakfast. Having inspected the kitchen, we walked back to the living room. I noted a sack behind a chair on which was a pile of old horse brass. Jai said that he had bought the lot cheap and was hammering it into shape and cleaning it up before selling it for a good price to an antique dealer. There were several cheap prints of nondescript country scenes hanging on the walls, but there was not a single book or magazine lying around.

'Was your father a gorgio?' I asked.

'Yes, he was,' he said abruptly.

We sat down on the bunk again. 'I can't remember him at all,' he went on. 'He was only around during the first year of my life.' He paused, then said without bitterness, 'I'm illegitimate.'

When Romanies talk of someone being illegitimate they mean that a couple has split up and gone separate ways and that one of the partners has disappeared and takes no interest in the other nor the welfare of any children born of the union. This is a rare occurrence, as I have said before, but the children seldom suffer from taunts of illegitimacy and a sense of shame.

'Did your mother marry later?' I asked.

'Yes, but she didn't have any more children. My eldest brother and me were born when she was living with this gorgio.'

'Did he leave her?'

'No, she left him. She's married to a Romany now.'

'I see.'

'My father wanted to keep one of us but my mother wouldn't let him. She was too fond of us to give one of us over to him, and besides she didn't care for the way gorgios bring up their chavvies.'

'Would you have liked to have been brought up as a gorgio?'

'Duw, no I don't care for the gorgio life at all.'

'It's not often that you find a Romany or didikai travelling and picking alone like you,' I said.

'I've only started going on my own this season. Before that I used to travel with my brother. He's a year older than me. But he's married now and I don't believe in traipsing round with a couple. Besides, I find being on my own pleasant enough, for a short while, anyway. I don't believe in living alone for too long, though. People become queer that way. You've only got to take one look at the mumpers and see what travelling alone has done to a lot of them. By the way, how many questions do you reckon you've asked me?'

'I'd say two or three.'

'I'd say close on ten. And so I'll ask you a few back. Where will you be going when the season ends?'

'I suppose I shall be going back to London,' I said. 'Strictly speaking, I should be in London now.'

'How's that?'

'I'm supposed to be at an art college but I'm not there very often.'

'No, you don't seem to be.'

'Some time ago I was awarded a grant by the London County Council to study painting for two years. I have attended the college quite a bit, but mostly I make excuses for not being there and get some other student to sign on for me. I do the same thing for some of them when I'm there and they feel like taking a little time off. One of these days, sooner or later – probably sooner – they'll find out and I shall be flung out and my grant discontinued. I never intended to become an artist,' I mused. 'I always meant to become a writer. But for reasons best known to those in the Ministry of Education, there are no grants for would-be writers. I use the allowance for travelling and writing and I do painting and drawing as a side-line.'

'A double life, in fact?'

'Very much of one.'

'How many people in London know that you're living with travellers?'

'No one. I keep my friends uninformed. This is my private life and I intend it to remain so.'

'I see,' he said slowly. 'I hope that you do keep it private, at least until you've decided one way or the other.'

'What do you mean?' I asked, 'one way or the other?'

He looked straight at me. 'I mean that one day you'll have to decide whether you'll return to the life you've left or stay along with me. I want you to come over here and live with me in the trailer. Later on, after you've had a fair time to get acquainted with the way I live, I'll ask you to rommer me. I'll be willing to go through a ceremony in a church or registry office if you'd prefer it that way. Years ago Mother had me and my brother christened in a Methodist chapel. I'd prefer a proper ceremony myself; I like getting these things tied down. Do you mind if I ask you a personal question? Have you had any affairs with men before you met me?'

'Nothing serious,' I said.

'I thought not. These things show through.' He looked at the swirling rain. 'It's a pity you're the one to do the deciding. It would be better if it were the other way about. Still, that can't be helped.' He regarded me with calm, prescient eyes. 'Well, will you be coming over, Reena?'

'Yes, I'll come,' I said.

'Is that a promise?'

'It is.'

'Kooshti. Get packed this evening, and I'll come and fetch you in the brake tomorrow morning.'

He got off the bunk and walked to the door. 'Bring the bike!' he called.

The children came running up in a bunch. I pulled the bike from a tow-headed boy and rode off.

Rain gurgled in the ditches and made the roadway glisten. Springing up from the long grasses growing on either side were buttercups and the torn pink petals of ragged-robin.

Turning a bend in the road, I almost ran over a black-and-white cat which was hurrying across with a mouse hanging from its jaws.

'You don't want to run over that cat – him's a real good mouser,' an old man called to me from the gateway of his cottage garden.

'Well, it should look out for traffic,' I said.

'Care for some peas?' asked the old fellow. 'I'm just shelling a few for my wife.'

'Peas!' I said, dismounting. 'I've had my fill of those during the past few weeks.'

'Well, these are garden peas, not field 'uns. And there's nothing that tastes better, in my opinion, than young raw peas fresh from the garden.'

He held a pod out. I shelled the pod and ate the contents.

'You working around here this season?'

'Yes. I'm staying with some travellers a few miles from here.'

'If ever you get the chance, and you're interested in such things,' he said, handing me another pod, 'go and visit that house near Wyre Piddle. It's set in the middle of large orchards on top of a hill. Nobody lives there now and the place is getting to be pretty shabby. It's quite small, two storeys, nothing much to look at. There's a pond in front where lots of old tins and ironmongery have been chucked.'

'Yes?'

'Well,' he continued, methodically shelling peas into a basin set on the wall, 'that house is haunted. You won't get many folks in the district going there after dark. There's a lot of paths winding through the orchards, and one woman who was picking there at dusk suddenly saw a figure gliding down a path towards her.'

'Wow!' I exclaimed.

'The woman didn't even say wow!' She just leapt down from the ladder and ran a good half mile till she got to the road. All sorts o' queer things happen there. Some people have seen a pale blue light shining from a room in the top storey. Other people say they've heard noises coming from the house and when they've climbed through a window and looked inside there's been nobody there.'

'Perhaps the ghost does a little picking occasionally and starts lugging sacks of apples round the house.'

He shrugged. 'The odd tramp used to spend the night there at one time. But now word's got about that the place is haunted they don't go there any more. Better a wet bed under a hedge than a dry one shared with a ghost, so it seems.'

At one time I used to be quite a keen amateur ghost hunter, but apart from a surfeit of poltergeists and several rather dim hauntings, nothing much of note came my way. The old man's account of hauntings in this house near Wyre Piddle aroused my curiosity in the supernatural once more and I made a mental note to visit it at the first opportunity.

When I got back, Thurzie and Euphryn were sitting on two chairs outside the tan. Euphryn had come to plead his case with Thurzie, but she remained adamant and refused to listen to him. My arrival did nothing to ease the tension. A black scowl appeared on Euphryn's face when he caught sight of me.

'Oh, Euphryn, you must have been arguing with me for close on an hour and I've said no, no, no! Will you go now, please,' Thurzie begged. 'There's no point in you stopping around any longer.'

'No, I guess there ain't. But afore I leave I want to find out when Reena's clearing off.'

'I'm clearing off tomorrow,' I said.

'Good! Morning or afternoon?'

'In the morning.'

'Reena, don't pay any attention to him,' said Thurzie. 'You're staying along here.'

I shook my head. 'I'm not leaving because of him,' I said. 'I've been very happy staying with you and your family, but I'm going away now.'

'Whatever for?'

'Jai's asked me to go along with him, and I've said that I will. He's coming to fetch me tomorrow morning in the brake.' Neither of them spoke for a moment. The scowl lifted from Euphryn's face.

'Jai!' he said, with some astonishment. 'But you only met him the other day and now you're talking about going off with him.'

'Reena, you're crazy!' said Thurzie. 'Do you mean that you and Jai are going to get rommerred or are you going to live with him a while?'

'I'll be travelling with him for a while,' I replied. 'Whether it will be for a long while or a short while, whether we'll get married or not I don't know, and neither does he. You must think I'm crazy, but what one person decides to do often strikes another as strange. Let's leave off talking about Jai and me. There are some things I can't explain to others and this is one of them.'

'Was it this afternoon he asked you to live with him?' Thurzie persisted.

'Yes, it was.'

'You should think things over a lot more, Reena, afore you go off with a man like that. You may be laying up a whole heap of trouble for yourself.'

'Maybe I am,' I said. 'But I've made my mind up. I've promised Jai to go over. There's nothing more to say.'

'Well, you're taking a big chance.'

'Don't worry about me, Thurzie. Jai's no shifty mumper.'

She said nothing more. Euphryn's expression had become sour and when he spoke his voice had a bitter quality. 'That's fine,' he said, 'you and Reena going off with Isidor and Jai, and I'm going to be left.'

'Duw! What a man you are. You wanted Reena to go off, didn't you? Well, just be pleased now that she is.'

'I'm pleased about her leaving,' he said grumpily. 'I'm just sorry about you and Isidor.'

His shoulders drooped and his voice was filled with self pity. My own unstated opinion was that Thurzie had had a lucky miss in not getting tied to him.

'You'll find someone else, Euphryn,' she said cheerfully. 'I know you will. Don't worry; you won't be alone for long. And now stop looking like an old broody hen.'

'I'd best be going or there'll be trouble,' said Euphryn abruptly, and he walked off across the field.

'I had to be sharp with him,' Thurzie explained, 'otherwise he'd be sitting there and moaning until the stars came out.'

That evening we heard that he got drunk at the pub and had to be escorted home by Tarsh and Hiram. Thurzie and I, sensing that Euphryn might cause trouble, had stayed behind. In consequence, I had to endure a long talk from Mrs Kizer after supper about the foolhardiness of the step I was about to take. But her talking had no effect on me. I was drawn ineluctably to Jai and nobody could have dissuaded me from going.

Sometimes you cannot hear a door closing on a period of your life, even if when you see a new door opening. It is only later that one comes to be aware of this. But when I bicycled away from Jai's trailer that afternoon I clearly heard with my inner ear a door closing behind me on my past life.

TEN

Home is Where the Heart is

THE FOLLOWING MORNING Jai came over for me in the brake as arranged and I left the Boswells to go and live with him in the trailer. Our days soon took on a similar pattern. During the picking season one rises early. We would get up about six-thirty and I would cook a good breakfast on the stove. Having eaten, Jai would do odd jobs outside the wagon while I did the housework. The big lurcher, Tom, would be let off the rope to take himself off for some exercise. Sometimes he got fighting with other dogs and Jai would have to run and separate the contestants. Whenever a dog fight occurs anyone in the vicinity hurries over to beat them apart no matter whose dogs they are. The thing is to get them separated quickly before they tear each other to bits. When the dogs are running loose they usually get on fairly well together, but it sometimes happens that they get into a brawl when one is leashed and the other free, and then the fight can be murderous if they are not pulled apart quickly. It is when they are leashed that they are most savage.

The housework finished, I would make up a large dish of bread and milk for Tom to start him off in good shape for the day. After his run he would be tied up again to the trailer, and then Jai and I would set off for the fields. We had started picking soft fruit now. This was not gruelling work. Sometimes we would return to the trailer at midday and have a snack lunch sitting on the steps. If we did, then Tom was lucky, for he would get his main meal then and would not have to wait for it till the late afternoon.

A few days after I had joined Jai we moved on to another farm along with the Fennets. Also at this farm were the Boswells' eldest daughter, Deborah, and her husband Tarsh.

Our hatchin-tan was in a field which adjoined an apple orchard and the trailer stood under some of the overhanging branches. At the other side of the field, against the hedge, the farmer had erected a tent for a mumper couple and their two children. The woman was quite a pleasant though rather a dim young slattern who hailed from Eire. Although her youngest child could barely toddle she was already heavily pregnant and would clearly be adding a third to her ragged family in the near future. The man she was with, father of the unborn child, was an uncouth flaxen-haired lout whose grimy speech was laced with obscenities. The children never knew where they were with their feckless parents and already had a dazed and anxious look on their small faces. One moment the woman would be calling them 'darling' and the man giving them playful smacks about their posteriors, and the next they would receive a vicious whack from one or the other for some trivial offence. This couple let their lousy little mongrel run loose most of the time, much to our annoyance, and it would come sniffing and snapping about one's ankles, retreating at once, tail between its legs, directly one turned and faced it.

'Get your bloody jukel tied up or make sure it keeps down your way,' Tarsh shouted at the man one afternoon as he was slouching across the field carrying two buckets of water. 'The next time it comes sneaking round here it gets its head knocked in.'

'You be careful else it'll be your head,' the man returned.

Tarsh walked straight up to him. 'Say that again!'

Immediately, man and dog backed away, with an oath and a snarl.

The evening meal, the big meal of the day, I always cooked in the open over the fire unless the weather was really bad. Deborah and I usually cooked a stew for four in one pot. The Fennets' iron pot would sometimes be hanging over our fire too, or ours over the fire they had lit. It just depended who got back first from the fields and whether or not we felt like eating in a group or by our own trailers or wagon, but mostly we ate together round the yog.

It was while we were eating thus one evening that we heard screams and groans coming from the other side of the field.

'Take no notice,' said Jai. 'It's just him giving her a clout over the head again.'

We carried on with the meal but the screams grew louder and more urgent. We could see the man standing at the tent opening, hands in pockets, saying something to the small girl, a child of about four. Then she started out towards us.

'Dordil What's up now?' said Deborah. 'He'd better not think that kid's going to get anything out of us.'

As though sensing the unfriendly atmosphere, the child stopped several yards from us and stared at the ground with downcast eyes.

'Go on!' the man bawled at her.

The child advanced a pace or two and, as we did not encourage her forwards by word or gesture, stopped again.

'You gone punk lame in one leg?' hollered the oaf from the other side of the field.

'What you come to beg?' Deborah asked the child.

'Nothing.'

'What you want then?'

'Bert says 'e wants you to come over and look at Ma.'

'Why?'

''Cos she's having a baby.'

'Struth!' said Tarsh, 'another poor little beggar,' and helped himself to a spoonful of stew.

'I'll have some more too,' said Isidor, taking the ladle from him.

We three women sighed and got up, leaving our meal half eaten.

'Have you got a pail of water bubbling on the yog?' Mrs Fennet asked the child. 'The fire,' she amended.

The child looked vague. 'Yes,' she answered, doubtfully.

'I bet,' said Mr Fennet.

'I'll follow you two over in a few minutes,' said Deborah. 'I must put Chrissie to bed first.'

I walked over to the tent with Mrs Fennet and Jai, who was carrying a pail of boiled water. Mrs Fennet had a clean knife and pot of Vaseline with her. I carried a small first-aid kit containing scissors, cotton wool, roller bandages, a tube of permanganate crystals, and sterilised plastic thread.

When we entered the tent, dimly lit by two candle stumps, the woman had stopped screaming and had set up a continuous low moan. She was lying on a sheet of tarpaulin and was covered by a scrofulous blanket. The tent was in an indescribable state of dirt and muddle; clothing, saucepans, food all piled up together. As Jai was putting down the bucket the slinking little mongrel came up from behind and gave him a sharp bite on the ankle. With considerable self control he said nothing, but flung the dog from the tent. For the first and only time, I saw a look of resentful apology on the man's face. We were, after all, on his side of the field, and it should have been only elementary courtesy, which he did not possess, to keep the dog off.

'Have you any clothes for the baby?' Mrs Fennet asked him.

He shook his head. There was not so much as a vest for the infant. The sheer fecklessness and beggarly-mindedness of this couple appalled me. They knew, as we knew, that they would manage to extract the few necessary bits and pieces of clothing from us.

As though in anticipation of the situation, when Deborah appeared she was carrying a bundle containing an old washed shirt torn up into large rags, a vest, flannel dress, cardigan, and a big square of flannel for a shawl, having known full well that nothing had been provided for the new life about to be born.

'What are you doing?' she asked me, shining the beam of a torch in my direction.

I was unrolling a two-inch bandage, while Mrs Fennet attended to the mother.

'That won't be needed,' said Deborah. 'You're wasting your time.'

I had once read up in a first-aid book the technique of dealing with a straightforward case of childbirth. All I lacked now that I was faced with a confinement was the one vital thing that counts in this world: experience.

'Go and get some more clean rags from somewhere,' Mrs Fennet told me. And I thankfully made my escape from the overcrowded and filthy tent. Although by no means a squeamish person, I was feeling quite sick and faint.

Two hours later I stood behind Mrs Fennet and Deborah, holding ready scissors and plastic thread, and witnessed the birth of this unfortunate infant. To say that I felt any sense of wonder at the drama of this particular human birth would be quite untrue. I was struck by the sordidness of everything and the grim life in store for the wailing scrap of a girl. I, like the Gypsies, am no sentimentalist. After mother and child had been made as clean and comfortable as possible under the circumstances, we all of us left the tent with sighs of relief, and returned to our mobile homes on the other side of the field feeling deeply thankful that our lives, though separated from theirs by only a short stretch of turf, were yet so different.

Jai was paring a short white stick when I entered the trailer, making a wood-shaving flower. Several large unpainted heads, with a hole at the unpetalled end, were lying on the table. I put them into a cardboard box.

'Boy or girl?' he asked.

'A girl.'

Warm night air blew through the open door and the windows. I stripped to the waist and washed outside under an apple tree in a bucket of cold water. A wind was rising, making the boughs of the tree knock gently against the trailer roof. I slid my fingers through the grass as Jai washed and dried my back.

'No picking tomorrow,' he said, emptying the contents of the bucket on to the ground. The last batch of chips filled with strawberries had gone into Stratford that afternoon.

'Let's go out somewhere in the brake,' I suggested. 'Take a day off.'

'Very well. But I must get those brasses over to the shop first. After that we can go somewhere, if you like.'

'There's a haunted house near Wyre Piddle,' I said.

'Duw! What on earth for – aren't there enough people around without you wanting to see ghosts as well?'

'It's a good excuse to take a trip down Evesham way,' I said.

The next morning Jai polished up the brasses for the last time, while I filled the thermos and put some food in a bag. Then we set off in the brake for Stratford.

Jai had managed to sell quite a lot of brasses to various shops in Wales and the Stratford area. There always seemed to be a demand for it, but every year it was getting more difficult. While he talked to the proprietor of an antique store, I went to the Post Office to collect my mail, delivered poste restante. All travellers collect their mail in this fashion. The C.P.O. is one of the few public bodies for which I have a feeling approaching affection. For years, whilst I travelled in Britain and lived in London digs, all my foreign and personal mail was sent regularly to this Post Office in Stratford. I would make regular journeys from wherever I happened to be, in order to collect it. Not once, so far as I am aware, was any mail lost. I have on many occasions while living in London – particularly in my last lodgings, a wretched room in Leytonstone – been truly thankful that in spite of the inconvenience I nevertheless kept to this arrangement.

Jai was already waiting for me by the brake when I returned with my mail and some groceries. He had made twelve bars (pounds) from the sale of the brasses.

Before leaving for Stratford that morning he had tied a piece of string round my fourth finger and knotted it. With this guide for measurement, he had bought, from another antique shop, a wide gold ring. I was to wear this ring all the time I was living with him.

'Where is this house you want to see?' he asked, as I dumped my shopping on to the back seat.

'Somewhere near Wyre Piddle,' I replied.

My vague directions as to the whereabouts of the house did not irk him as they might have done a gorgio. He took life calmly. When we reached the small village of Wyre Piddle I spotted an old mumper woman pushing a pram.

'Ever heard of a haunted house round these parts?' I asked her, leaning from the brake window.

'It's closer Evesham way,' she replied, digging a finger in the direction of that town. 'Down the road and up in those orchards by that hill.'

A few more enquiries brought us to the orchards. We parked the car and, after some minutes' walking, came to the house which stood in an open clearing surrounded by fruit trees.

Most of the panes in the windows had been broken and some of the windows had been boarded up. There was an air of desolation about the place. The 'pond', a sunken, muddy hole, looked as if it had been a pickers' and picnickers' garbage disposal pit for years. We peered into the lower rooms of the house and walked round the building. Then we continued onwards down a track which led out of the orchards and on to a grassy hillside. Here we sat down and I opened the parcel of food. Jai took out his wallet and counted through the notes. With our earnings from picking for the week, together with the money for the brasses, the sum came to £25.

'We'll keep these bars for spending and I'll not touch the money in the box till winter,' he said.

He had £150 in a tin box which was kept in a larger wooden box with a padlock to it. With this money, and whatever else could be put by during the course of the season, he intended to start a second-hand chopping mart for brakes and cars at Bristol. He saw himself clearing several hundred pounds before late spring, when he would take to the road once more in a new brake. His present one had a good engine but was decidedly shabby about the body. It was to be his first chop to start the business going. The whole scheme sounded pretty crazy to me, but I said nothing to discourage him.

We lay down on the short, dry grass, the wind blew over us. 'Have you decided yet?' he asked.

I did not reply immediately. 'Come on, answer,' he said.

'No, I haven't decided yet. Give me a while longer.'

'Just how much longer do you expect me to wait? I've bought you a ring. I've said I'll marry you in a church if you prefer it that way, and –'

'Yes, I know. But our lives have been so different. I'm afraid that one day these differences may pull us apart.'

'You're too pessimistic. Why shouldn't the things we have in common keep us together? You've seen the way I live. You've told me you don't care for the life you live in London. We love each other. Doesn't all that mean something and make it simple for you to decide?'

'You make everything sound so easy, Jai, but it's not. I must ask you to give me longer in which to make up my mind.'

'Oh, hell!' he said angrily. 'We'll both be dead and buried afore you make up your mind at the rate you're going. What's so difficult about coming to a decision, one way or the other what's holding you up?'

I could not explain. There were so many things that were almost a necessity to me and which I would virtually have to give up if I stayed with him for good: books, foreign travel, art, and much more besides. These things had never touched his life and he felt no need for them.

'Have you ever wanted to go abroad?' I asked, tentatively, trying to put my position more clearly to him by talking of a subject in which at least he took a certain interest – travel, albeit it on the home ground.

'You've gone right off the track,' he said. 'I asked what was holding you up?'

'Well, in my question lies a small part of the answer.'

'No, I haven't wanted to go abroad. England and Wales are good enough for me.'

'I should like to go. For years I've promised myself that one day I'll travel out East again to India.'

'Where?'

'A country in Asia.'

'Asia?'

'Oh, Jai!' I exclaimed in exasperation. 'Don't tell me you haven't heard of Asia?'

'Of course I have, but I don't know whereabouts it is. And anyway, wherever it is, there's no point in you going there now that you've met me.' He glanced at my mail lying on the grass. 'What's all these letters with foreign stamps on – who are they from?'

He picked up a letter and ripped open the envelope, spreading out the thin airmail paper. 'Who's this from – someone in India? Read it out.'

'Not on your life. See what comes of not being able to read?' I went on, unwisely. 'I'll be able to keep all my interesting sappengro boyfriends' news from you.'

'Maybe I'll keep their news from you. I don't care if these letters come from boyfriends or from some chimp in the jungle. It doesn't make no difference, because I'm going to put an end to all this foreign letter writing.' And with that he started tearing the letters up.

'Oh, please don't, Jai!' I begged. 'I was only teasing you. Those letters don't come from any boyfriends, but from plain, ordinary people living abroad. I promise you.'

He pushed me away as I tried to get hold of them, and continued ripping them up. When each one was torn to shreds he flicked on his lighter and burnt the pile of unread mail.

'And now,' he said, scattering the ashes to the wind, 'let's eat. Don't go into one of your brooding moods. I can't stand artistic temperament.

What's in this sandwich cheese and pickles?'

'There have been one or two occasions in my life,' I said, as evenly as I could, 'when I've longed for more physical strength, just so that I could give some self-centred male a really hard clout.'

'Don't waste your energy. It's no good longing for what you can never have. It's a woman's job in life to get her way by being subtle, not by using her fists.'

'Subtle! There'd be little point in trying to be subtle with you. That would be water off the proverbial duck's back.'

'Did you bring any lettuce?' he asked.

My temper cooled gradually. After I had eaten I stood up and looked across the Evesham Valley. Behind us were the orchards with their winding tracks and before us the open expanse of valley.

'Let's take a walk to the end of the hill,' I suggested. 'We can leave the things here till we get back.'

We walked across the hill, our arms about each other's waists, up a few steps and down, in a slow zig-zag. Suddenly Jai stopped.

'I've forgotten something,' he said.

'What?'

'My wallet. I left it lying on the ground.'

'Never mind; it'll be safe. There's no one about.'

'Let's turn back all the same.'

He slipped his arm from my waist and started back over the sloping ground with quick strides. 'What's the hurry?' I called. He was several paces ahead of me when he reached the spot where we had been sitting. I saw him lift up some paper bags, then the thermos. He let out an exclamation. 'It's gone!' he said.

'Oh, it can't be gone! Where did you put it last?'

'Here – by this bag.'

The grass was not thick and it was a matter of seconds to see that the wallet was not on the patch of ground. 'Look in your pockets, Jai,' I said. 'You must have put it back in one and forgotten.'

He shook his head as he put his hands into his jacket and trouser pockets. 'It's no use,' he said. 'I remembered as we were walking along that I had left it lying on the grass, and when I did I got a curious feeling. I knew all of a sudden that someone had been watching us and had taken it.'

'But we were only gone a couple of minutes.'

'Two minutes too long. Come, follow me, quick. I'm going to run back to that house. Maybe the thief's hiding there.'

'There's a few acres of orchards, too, where he could be hiding.'

I suddenly felt very uneasy or, to be more exact, fearful.

'Quick!' he called.

Already he was yards ahead of me. I saw him swerve right, away from the open hillside, and race along the track, bordered by fruit trees, which led back to the desolate, ruined house. By making a great effort, I managed to catch up with him and I tugged hard at his jacket.

'Don't,' I gasped, 'don't go into that house, please, Jai. Forget about the money. It's gone now.'

He stopped running just before he reached the clearing, and said in a low voice: 'Wait for me here under the trees. Don't come any further.'

'If you must go in, take a heavy stone or something with you. He may have a knife.'

'Don't worry. I won't be needing any stitching together. Wait here. . .'

He ran off past the pond and I watched him climb through a window.

I stood under a heavily leafed plum tree. I could see the top storey of the house through the leaves, but as yet no sign of Jai at a window. I looked upwards at the greenery. Some of the fruit was a deep red. In under a month, unless the weather broke, it would be purple and ready for picking. I raised a hand and touched a plum just ahead of me. As I did so I became aware, with a sense of shock, of a dark figure standing to my left. I knew without looking round that it was the figure of a man and that he was watching my movements. The thief was not hiding in the house but was standing here, almost beside me. Slowly I lowered my arm, then turned my head to look at him. The impression I received of him during those seconds in which we looked into one another's eyes was vivid and precise. Years later I was able to summon up his image at will and it would still be as vivid as on this first occasion.

He was of medium height, well built, dressed in a navy-blue suit with a white shirt buttoned up to the neck, and no tie. On his head he wore a black trilby hat which cast a shadow over the upper portion of his face, yet did not hide the features. He had a smooth, perfect skin, and high cheekbones, yet there was nothing feminine or oriental about his appearance. His mouth was wide and rather flat. Straight black hair was brushed away from the smooth forehead. His eyes never shifted or wavered an instant as they looked into mine; they gave me an impression of dark pools which the sunlight never reached. When our eyes first met, he smiled slightly as though in acknowledgment of my fear, and then, almost idly, he took a step forward and, imitating the way I had raised my hand up to the plum, raised his own towards my throat.

Something – some slight sound or movement – caught his attention. He looked round, then bending his body a little to avoid a branch, ran off slowly and silently between the trees.

I found that I was holding my throat with both hands to protect it from his grip. I walked out from under the branches. Jai came running up and I slumped against him.

'I spotted him from a top window,' he said. 'Did he hurt you? What's he done to your throat?'

I shook my head to show that I had not been hurt. The power of speech had temporarily left me. Presently I regained some composure. Jai was looking about him. 'Don't go after him – oh, please don't!' I begged him again. 'We'll make up the money somehow.'

'All right,' he said.

On the drive back to camp we said little. My nerves were still on edge from my encounter with the thief, and when a feather blew in through the window I started violently.

When we related the events to the rest of the group round the fire that evening, Mr Fennet waited for us to finish and then told us a curious tale.

That very morning, just before we had left for Stratford, he and Isidor had gone off to cut a bundle of wood for flower-making. This job done, Isidor had spent the rest of the day visiting Thurzie, and Mr Fennet had gone to a pub in Long Marston, where he had met up with some travellers he knew.

'That man who pinched your wallet will be the same chap as the Lukes and Mobsies were telling me about in the pub,' he said to Jai. 'He's been to several farms roundabouts, though just what for, nobody knows, for he don't seem to go for the picking – not fruit and vegetables, anyway. Well, he arrives at the farm the Lukes and Mobsies were at latish one evening, wearing the same clothes Reena saw him in – dark suit, white shirt, and black hat. He told two mumper fellows in a tan that he'd been taken on by the farmer, which he hadn't been, and that he was coming to share the tan with them. "Three in this tan?" they says. The man just shrugs his shoulders and sits down. "I'll be making myself scarce most of the time," he says. That sounded a bit odd, and there was something about the man they didn't care for at all. Dick Mobsie was washing his hands under the tap in the yard when this chap – although he weren't a Romany, Dick didn't call him a gorgio neither –'

'If he weren't a Romany and weren't a gorgio, then what was he – a foreigner?' asked Hiram.

Mr Fennet ignored the question and continued. 'The chap didn't say anything to Dick, just put his hands under the running water and looked at him. "And the way he looked at me gave me a queer start," Dick said. "When I got back to the vardos I told everyone that a mokardo had arrived and we had better get him away before nightfall."'

The word 'mokardo' is rarely used by the Gypsies. It means depraved, and this was the only time I heard them apply it to an individual within their immediate kin.

'Six of the men,' Mr Fennet continued, 'went across to the tan. The two mumpers were sitting apart from the mokardo, and he was doing a bit of cooking over the yog. "We've come to tell you to clear off," says Curtis Luke. The mokardo never looks at them, just turns some chips over in the pan. "Why?" he asks. He had an educated sort of voice.

"Just let's say we don't like the look of you," says Curtis. The man smiles, puts a hand in his trouser pocket and pulls out a long, foreign-looking knife. "I got this in Spain," he says, laying it on the ground beside him. At that, everyone of the men brought out a blade of some sort. The mumpers came over from the side of the tan where they'd been squatting and sat next to the others. They added their penknives to the blades already on display. "You've got twenty minutes," says Dick, "to eat and then clear off." They sat round him, waiting. He ate his supper, leant back on an elbow and fingered his blade. Curtis looked at his watch – "Five minutes!" Dick says he stared hard at the man all this while. He had pushed his hat right to the back of his head, but there was something neat and finicky about his appearance, and he looked as though he took a good wash now and then.'

'Were he a foreigner?' asked Isidor.

'No, he was English all right. Just afore the five minutes were up Dick asks him what part of the country he comes from. "Let's say Liverpool," he answers. "This your first season picking?" "I don't believe in soiling my fingers," he replies. And Dick said that when he took a good look at the man's hands he knew that he had meant what he said, for they were very smooth with the nails in good shape. Then Curtis gave a sign and the six fell on the man while the two mumpers gripped him by the feet. He was carried across the field to the roadway like a trussed hen. They gave him a few knocks about the chest just to make sure he knew he wasn't welcome and someone ran back for his pack and flung it after him. "Don't try mixing with Romanies again," Dick called, as the mokardo lifted the pack on to his shoulder. "If you do, they'll move you on so quick you'll break the sound barrier." "Can I have my knife back?" he asks, very polite. "Oh, no; we're holding on to that!" He says nothing more and walks off. They buried the knife in the field. Even the mumpers said they didn't fancy having it. Let's hope he's moved from the district now.'

'You mean, now that he's pinched my bars,' said Jai. 'Whoever he is, he hasn't done so bad. There were twenty-five of them in my wallet.'

'If I was you and that money was returned to me,' said Isidor, 'I wouldn't lay a finger on it. I'd burn it straightway.'

'Kooshti duw! I'm not that superstitious. I'd like the money back and him with it, so that I could give him a hard kick in the rump and then rub his nose in the dust.'

It never occurred to anyone in the group, with the exception of myself, to inform the police about the theft. Jai would have put no faith in them recovering the money. But apart from that, travellers have never been on very amicable terms with the constabulary. The Romany of today, as of yesterday, still prefers to deal with his own affairs in the way he thinks best, without assistance or interference from outsiders, particularly when the outsider happens to be a policeman.

ELEVEN

A Rommerrin

ISIDOR BOUGHT A GOOD second-hand trailer with a car to tow it, and it was pitched next to ours. He put down £300 for the trailer and over £200 for the car. His parents and the Boswells helped him a little with the payments, but most of the money he had saved himself. The trailer had everything to delight the heart of a modern Gypsy chie, and Thurzie confessed that she was thrilled with it. The rommerrin ceremony was to take place at the Boswells' field next Saturday.

I have often been surprised at the comparative wealth – taken at the travellers' level – of many Gypsy families. Not only do they own a good deal of mobile property as well as gold jewellery, china, bedding, animals, birds and so forth, but they often keep several hundred pounds in five-pound notes in the kitty, to tide them over spells of unemployment or to make a good buy. It may often happen that a family may be completely broke for a few days or weeks, but they are seldom broke for very long, and they have their own homes in which to brood over their penury. They cannot be turned out of lodgings at a week's notice, which is often the fate of townspeople at the mercy of landladies. If a family gets into real financial difficulties there is nearly always a relation or friend willing to lend them money. But it is a spineless family indeed which cannot earn a few coins by hawking or chopping something during lean periods. I asked Mrs Fennet whether she had ever known a homeless Gypsy family who had had to sell their wagon through lack of funds and not been able to afford a cheap replacement. She said that she had known this to happen on one or two occasions, but the family without a wagon were always given temporary quarters in someone else's. The quarters would naturally be very cramped, but at least no Gypsy family would be sleeping under the hedgerow.

Thurzie came over one evening, dressed in a new blouse and skirt, in order to do a few chores around her future home. Every Gypsy girl, and most of the older women, keep a few items of 'best' clothing for special occasions and for when they are courting. White frilled or flowered blouses are very popular with the younger women nowadays. And brightly coloured silk headscarves and shawls are still much worn.

Thurzie sat in our trailer drinking a cup of tea. She had quite accepted the idea of Jai and me living together and told me that she thought we made a good pair. She was looking very pretty in a new mock tartan skirt and fresh white blouse with a square neckline. Her hair had been recently permed ready for her wedding. It had been a home perm. I had read out the instructions to her and she had repeated them exactly to Mrs Kizer who at her first attempt – tongs dispensed with – had made an excellent job of her daughter's hair.

Thurzie had brought with her a tiny pair of earrings as a present from Mrs Kizer to her granddaughter Chrissie; for the time had come for Chrissie's ears to be pierced with a darning needle. Neither Thurzie nor Deborah seemed at all concerned about the child's forthcoming ordeal.

As I looked from a window, she was sitting in her pram playing with a rattle, unaware of what lay ahead of her.

Tarsh entered, looking somewhat disgruntled. 'I always take myself off,' he said to no one in particular, 'before the women start to pierce the girls' ears.'

'We chies don't mind,' said Thurzie, holding out the earrings.

'They're very nice,' said Tarsh briefly, helping himself to tea from the pot. 'I don't suppose I'll get much sleep tonight with Chrissie squalling in her cradle.'

'Don't be so daft!' said Thurzie. 'She'll have stopped squalling afore you go to bed. Ma says I hardly let out a whimper when I had my ears pierced.'

'Go on!' said Tarsh.

'Well, that's what she says. But Deb, now, she –' Thurzie stood up.

'Deborah did, I suppose you was going to say. There's no need for you to hide Deb's failings. I bet you both bawled your heads off, whatever Ma Kizer may say. Poor little Chrissie. . .'

'Don't worry yourself about her, Tarsh; she'll be all right. Men are ever so soft about some things – don't you think so, Reena? They aren't half so brave when it comes to a little operation on themselves or their chavvies. Then they come over queer in a minute. Women, now, you won't get them turning the colour of a lettuce leaf at a mere pinprick. Are you coming over to watch, Reena?'

'No, thanks,' I said hurriedly. 'There are one or two jobs that need doing in the trailer.'

Thurzie left and Jai and Tarsh looked at me intently, but I did not bat an eyelid, though I had an idea that I had gone several shades paler at the thought of what Chrissie was to endure in a few minutes' time.

Presently we heard high-pitched yells, followed by soothing words from the women, then Thurzie appeared at the doorway and flung bloody water from an enamel bowl. The yells gradually softened to whimpers and Deborah called out to her husband that it was all over and Chrissie had stood the ordeal well. The next morning the child was out in her pram as usual, looking none the worse and with the gold earrings through the lobes of her small ears.

During the days which followed the weather turned really hot. I worked in an old cotton blouse and linen skirt, while most of the men worked stripped to the waist. I encouraged Jai in this habit as it meant washing fewer shirts. Almost every day I would boil up a big pot of water and do some of the laundry, hanging it out on the trees to dry. If the wash consisted of small articles like handkerchiefs I would peg them out on the kitchen line.

When Jai was sitting on the steps one evening, thumbing through an illustrated weekly I had bought, and I was wringing out some clothes by the trailer, I happened to catch sight of the mumper woman coming out of the tent. Although she had not begun working again in the fields she was now up and about. In fact, she had got up on the second day after the child was born. I watched her walk slowly from the tent, followed by the small girl, and spread a few bits and pieces of washing on the hedge which were handed to her by the child. If she had been a Gypsy the husband and other women relatives would have taken over the everyday tasks for a period, lent a hand with the children, gone shopping for her, done the washing and cooking, and most likely she would have spent a full week in bed. But this woman, with two small children and a new-born infant, had to fend for herself.

'It's too bad,' I remarked to Jai. 'She's been and done some washing and that lazy oaf, Bert, is just lying on his back asleep.'

'Well, that's something, isn't it – she's got him lying around?'

'Really, Jai, the way you speak at times makes me furious!'

He continued to glance through the paper, then said, 'There was no need for her to take him on if she didn't want to. Maybe with his child on the way and two others fathered by different men she reckoned that half a man was better than none, and I think she was right. He's earning cash in the fields and does a hand's turn about the tan now and then. Where would she be better off – in some home for the down and out?'

'I'm not so sure she wouldn't be. At least she'd have proper attention for a while and her children would be looked after for her, and taken off her hands so that she could have a good rest. Every woman deserves that much.'

'It's not what you deserve in this world, it's what you get, and what you make or don't make for yourself out of life. If you've got nothing you're miserable, and if you've got too much you're probably miserable too, but you must have something to call your own. She's got three kids and a man. I don't mind betting she's a good deal happier than many women who live alone in a room and work all day in an office or a factory. I know more about these mumper women than you do,' he went on. 'In one of those institutions or homes, so called, the first thing they do is separate the family; the man's never allowed along with the woman, the children are put in some other place away from the mother. All these homes are like nunneries and monkeries; strict segregation of the sexes, and the old separated from the young. And it's quite likely, if the authorities think that the woman isn't living the life of some sainted aunt, and not many of them are, they may take her children away from her for good. Maybe they'll find her some sort of a job and give her another chance later on to have the children back. But if they decide to take the kids from her and the man deserts her, then she hasn't got very much left. Sometimes I've heard people say the kids are often better off in a home. Well, maybe they are and maybe they're not. It just depends. But don't go worrying yourself about her over there. There's a lot of women a darn sight worse off than she is.'

Nevertheless, I was somewhat perturbed about the mumper woman and later on I walked over to the tent with a bowl of cooked potatoes, half a sponge roll, and a packet of tea. I enquired after the baby.

'Oh, she's doing nicely, thanks,' said the woman.

The couple were quite pleasant for a change and we chatted together amicably. I noticed that there was a large jug of milk on the ground.

'Here,' I said, 'break up some of this jam sponge into a bowl and pour some milk over it. That'll make a nice meal for the children.' I meant, of course, for the two eldest.

The man at once started pulling off pieces of sponge and dropping them into a mug, then poured some milk over them, while the children waited eagerly for this treat.

'Steady now,' he said, 'one at a time.'

Each in turn took a piece of soggy sponge from the mug with a grubby little hand and gulped it down.

'Here, give me a bit,' said the woman.

I thought she was going to try a piece herself, but no, she pinched open the sleeping infant's mouth and dropped in a small bit.

'Take it out!' I cried. 'She'll choke.'

'It's been well soaked; she can manage,' was the laconic reply.

'She's much too young for any food,' I said in alarm.

The woman peered into the baby's mouth, but the piece of sponge had disappeared. The baby spluttered, wrinkled up its face and looked as though it were going to choke to death. At last it managed to get the sponge down and started a thin, even bleat.

'Don't give it any more sponge,' I entreated, and returned to the trailer.

'Can you believe it?' I said to Jai. 'She's had two children already, yet she can do a thing like that.'

'I believe it,' he said. 'If you aren't careful, you can do a lot more harm than good with those people. My advice to you is to let them get on by themselves as best they may and don't go trotting over there with any more sponges and packets of tea.'

Some of Jai's pronouncements often seemed hard to me, but months or even years later I often came to accept, by and large, much of what he said.

The Romany wedding, or rommerrin, is not such a colourful affair now as it used to be, judging from accounts. When I asked Thurzie whether she and Isidor were going to jump over the yog together, hand in hand, she replied that that particular custom had gone out of fashion long ago. Even so, I was to find that quite a lot of the traditional wedding ceremony was still being observed.

On the Friday evening before the wedding I washed my hair and put it in curlers, and ironed out my blouse and Jai's shirt and scarf. We had given the couple an embroidered tablecloth and a gold link bracelet for Thurzie. Gold, in some form or other, is considered lucky.

On Saturday afternoon we set off in the brake, which was filled to overflowing with other travellers besides ourselves. The bridegroom and his relatives drove on ahead in Isidor's new car.

A big crowd had gathered in the Boswells' field, many of whom I had not seen before. We had brought along with us, as had most of the others, our own plates, mugs and cutlery for the supper which would follow the ceremony.

All the women were wearing gold jewellery, their best blouses and skirts, and many had shawls flung over their shoulders and had tied silk scarves, Gypsy style, round their heads. The children were in a variety of costumes, from the latest Marks and Spencer nylon dresses and jersey suits to well-worn cottons and jumpers which had been passed from older children down to the younger ones. Many of the small girls were wearing headscarves and jewellery like the women, and their hair had been set in elaborate waves and curls for the occasion.

Over the doorway of the Boswells' wagon was nailed a piece of yellow furze – the Gypsies' flower – and buckets filled with it had been placed at the head of the circle we formed. Here stood the young couple and close relatives. Thurzie looked surprisingly demure as she waited beside her groom for the ceremony to begin.

The rommerrin started off with speeches. Mr Boswell said that Thurzie had been the best of daughters, much loved by her parents, brother and sister, and he was very pleased that she had chosen such a fine young man as Isidor for a husband. He thanked the many relatives and friends present for coming along and asked them to join with him in wishing the pair health, happiness and long lives, and herewith he handed Thurzie over into Isidor's safe keeping.

It was now Mr Fennet's turn. He welcomed the bride into his family, and said he was sure everyone present would agree that his son had done very well for himself. He, too, thanked relatives and friends for coming along, many from far afield, and voiced his wishes for the health and happiness of his son and daughter-in-law.

Then Hiram stepped up alongside Thurzie, and Mr Fennet's nearest relative, a brother, stood by Isidor. They both carried a knife and made a short gash across the right wrist of bride and groom. As the blood started to flow, Thurzie turned her arm so that her palm and Isidor's touched, then Hiram tied a white handkerchief round their wrists, uniting them. When the blood had mingled and a large patch of the handkerchief was stained red it was untied and a small piece of adhesive tape and a narrow bandage placed round each wrist to staunch the flow. The pair were now wedded. They were immediately besieged by well-wishers, and Isidor was given many resounding smacks on the back, which he accepted good-naturedly. There followed much talking and laughter while the women relatives of the bride started to get the meal ready.

It was a really good feast, with beer, cider and lemonade to drink. The main dish, which had been cooked in half a dozen large iron pots, was a rich game stew, chiefly pheasant, though one pot was full of hare. The vegetables – potatoes, onions, carrots, turnips, all well seasoned with parsley, mint and thyme – had been cooked separately. Just where the birds and hares had been acquired I had no intention of asking, but they certainly had not been purchased from the farmer or local butcher. Thurzie had asked Mrs Kizer if she might have a real wedding cake, and Mrs Kizer and Fanny had gone into Stratford and bought two large cakes with frosted icing. These were now cut up and handed round, every man, woman and child receiving a piece.

Rommerrins are popular, not only for the ceremony itself, but also because Gypsies come from miles away to attend them, so that the latest bits of news and gossip about friends and relatives travelling in other parts of the country can be exchanged. It often happens that people who have not seen each other for years meet again at a rommerrin. Gypsies are always well up on the latest news concerning themselves, in spite of the fact that they write few letters and read fewer papers.

The talk that day, as we ate the wedding supper, was of the travelling life, of deals that had been made, the police and their interfering ways, rates of pay for pickers that season, hawking, animals, wagons and trailers. Listening, I was certain the talk had changed little through the centuries, ever since the Gypsies first arrived in Europe during the sixteenth century.

As it started to grow dusk mugs were emptied, scraps were thrown to the dogs, and the crowd began to disperse. Many of the families who had come from a distance wanted to get back to their camping ground for a few hours' sleep before commencing the day's work in the fields, for Sunday is not always a day of rest during the picking season.

It was quite late by the time the newly-weds were escorted back to their trailer by a crowd of young relatives. No one was actually drunk, but the noisy laughter and jesting that went on at the couple's expense was extremely rowdy and would have proved trying to a pair of gorgios. Several times Thurzie and Isidor mounted the steps only to be pulled back by several young males who swore they were not going to let them inside. But at last they gained entrance and slammed and locked the door behind them. I thought that there is a good deal to be said for the gorgio honeymoon, when a newly-wedded couple get right away by themselves for a spell.

After Thurzie and Isidor had made their escape, many of the crowd came and hammered on our door, and there was nothing to do but let them in. Deborah knocked on a window and asked me to boil up the kettle and make some tea, then she hurried back to her trailer to get her own kettle on the boil. It seemed the feasting and merry-making were not yet over. I pushed my way to the kitchen through a crowd of noisy travellers and lit the gas ring. People followed me in, interested to inspect every inch of the trailer. Not wishing to appear a reluctant hostess – though I found it difficult to believe that anyone would want more food – I opened the cupboard and brought out a loaf of bread and a Dundee cake which fortunately I had in stock. This was more of a gesture on my part, but to my surprise the loaf was taken from me by a woman who started to cut it up, enquiring at the same time for butter, and there were general exclamations of approval at the sight of the cake.

I delved once again into the cupboard and brought out two jars of jam and some sandwich spread. 'Would anyone care for cheese with their bread?' I asked.

'Yes, please!' came a chorus, so I unwrapped a hunk of cheddar.

Deborah and Tarsh appeared with trays laden with cups of tea and eatables, and once more we started to drink, eat and exchange gossip.

A large fire had been lit in the field and as the evening wore on a crowd gathered around it. Some of the guests who were not working the following day had received permission from the farmer to pitch their trailers in our field for the night. The only persons who did not put in an appearance round the fire were the newly-weds, who wisely stayed locked inside their trailer. The sky darkened and the flames grew brighter and leapt higher. Someone started to play an accordion and sing, but the voluble chatter continued unabated. Between the flaming logs and the tight-packed circle of people, several pet dogs and a hen had managed to wedge a passage and were busy searching for scraps.

The thought struck me as I sat there that our store-cupboard was cleaned out and we had nothing to eat for breakfast or lunch. My preoccupation with food after the way we had eaten verged on gluttony, but as a gorgio I had been brought up to keep a stock of it in hand. The Gypsies are extraordinarily happy-go-lucky concerning food for the morrow and the laying in of adequate supplies.

'You take your muzzle away from me 'cause you ain't going to get nothing,' came Mrs Fennet's voice as she addressed some dog. 'No good you thinking you are – here, then, take this bit of cheese and away with you.'

I wondered whether she was feeling a little sad now that her only son was married and happily installed in his trailer with his bride. If she was, she did not show it and talked and joked away with the best of them.

I began to get drowsy. Night had descended, but people seemed unaware of the lateness of the hour and continued their conversations as animatedly as before. Bits of their talk drifted to my ears and were swept away again.

'. . .one of the best hatchin-tans in that part of the country. We pitched right up against the pine strip and had the river in front of us. Never any trouble about water. . .'

'Where's this hatchin-tan?' somebody asked.

The reply was drowned in a babble of voices.

'We still goes there . . . sometimes leave you in peace for as long as five days. But there ain't many houses around for the women to call at. Just one or two little cottages set in the hills.'

'That jukel, him's a cross between a whippet and a fox – swear to God he is. This dog's Ma was tied to the vardo and we was sitting a way off, when we see this old dog fox go up to her . . . cunning, you can't put nothing over him . . . takes after his Dad in that way . . . dark grey back, with a red muzzle and chest. . .'

The scene had a timeless quality about it: the animated faces illuminated by the firelight, while overhead the stars appeared and disappeared as the night clouds passed over them.

Beside me, Jai leant on an elbow. His eyes were closed and his long lashes touched his cheeks. He held a lighted cigarette and every so often blew a stream of smoke from between his lips. I looked at him intently for a few seconds as though he were a stranger. Whatever there was of gorgio blood in him had been obliterated by the stronger Romany blood and years – all his years – of living the travelling life. Without turning his head or opening his eyes, he realised that I was regarding him and he gave me a dig with his elbow by way of informing me to stop. Anything that could be interpreted as a show of affection in public was anathema to him, as it is to many Romanies, and he held that all forms of love-making should be kept for the privacy of the wagon. It was a view which largely coincided with my own.

A small child was sound asleep, its head resting on its knees. The mother gave it a light cuff over the ears and told it to get along to bed. Gradually people started to leave the firelight. I laid my hand upon the hen's back. It had gone to sleep within almost a foot of the flames and its feathers were too hot for me to keep my hand there with any comfort. Hens, like cats, thoroughly enjoy getting really well toasted when the chance to do so comes their way.

As we walked to the trailer, Jai said, 'You'll get a surprise when you open the door.'

And, sure enough, I did.

He had bought a cage of linnets from one of the visiting Gypsies and smuggled it inside when I was out. The birds blinked and unfolded their wings when the lamp was lit. I found a piece of cloth and put it over the cage.

Jai looked out at the dark shape of the trailer drawn up close to ours. Its lights were out, the bridal couple gone to bed.

'They're fixed up for life,' he commented, 'and that's what I want.'

I said nothing, and went and sat down in front of the mirror and started to brush my hair. I heard him sigh deeply.

'Give me to the end of this year, Jai. I won't ask for any more time after that, I promise you, and I won't compromise either. I'll say yes or no; I'll stay with you always, or goodbye.'

It was his turn to say nothing.

The hands of the alarm clock pointed to three. Jai picked up a cowboy paperback which I was reading to him in the evenings, chapter by chapter.

'Here,' he said, 'I'll brush your hair, and then let's have one chapter before we go to bed.'

'Where did we get to?' I asked, after my hair had been brushed and combed to his satisfaction. Every chapter seemed more or less the same to me; one long shooting match of flying bullets, arrows and tomahawks, and blood-curdling war-whoops.

'Surely you remember; the hero's lying wounded in a canyon and has just spotted a thin column of smoke in the distance, but he don't know yet whether it's from a White's or an Indian's fire. Go on – much further on than that,' he said, as I flicked over the pages uncertainly.

I started to read out a bit – 'As he lay on the hard stones and watched the thin plume ascending in the distance – yes?'

'That's it. Carry on.'

'It seemed to Orvil to be an omen – good or bad – he didn't know yet. Only a raving optimist would have rated him a chance in a thousand. Without a mount, no water, and his right leg out of action, he had to admit that his prospects of getting out of the canyon alive did not appear too bright. . .'

It was close on four when I finished reading. There was to be no picking that Sunday. We lay in bed till ten and then got up for a cup of tea. There was, of course, nothing to eat.

TWELVE

A Double Life

MID-WAY THROUGH THE SEASON it became necessary for me to return for a while to London. It was high time that I did. The student at my art school who had been signing on for me was going to the Cornish Riviera to do a little painting and relaxing at Mousehole, while I duly signed his name on the attendance sheets.

Before setting off to the school from my lodgings next morning, I applied a heavy white make-up over my suntanned complexion and ringed my eyes with grey shadow. The effect was ghastly, and as I peered at my reflection in the mirror I wondered whether I had not rather overdone it. Whenever I put in brief appearances at the school I always took care to make myself as wan-looking as possible; should my confederate have omitted for some reason to have signed on for me, I should be able to explain my absence as due to ill health.

The life classes at this school were vast and it was precisely for this reason that I had put my name down for them. Often as many as forty or fifty students attended them at a time. The two masters, looking infinitely bored as they leant against the wall talking to each other, would sometimes go over to one of the more promising pupils, while the rest were left to fend for themselves. This suited me perfectly.

The first morning back I walked briskly through the hall and, with a certain amount of trepidation, entered the office to ask for my grant money. The chief clerk looked at me intently.

'Ah, yes, Miss Farre, I've been meaning to speak to you.'

My heart sank.

'You should have signed for your money last week, but you did not do so and nobody seemed to know where you were. However, that is not the only thing I wish to mention. We have been going through the attendance sheets and find that there are several missing signatures against your name. Why is that?'

'Er, yes, I'm afraid there are,' I said quickly sinking in to the nearest chair, pressing a hand to my forehead. 'I haven't been very well lately.'

'How many days have you been absent?'

'Oh, just one or two.'

'One or two!' He removed a card from a tray. 'Five days in all not signed for.'

'Is that so? Yes, now I come to think of it, I suppose I must have been away about five days,' and I gave a hacking cough. 'Pardon me. I'm still not quite –'

'Why didn't you ring us up if you were ill, or send a doctor's certificate?'

'Well, there's no phone at my lodgings and I didn't think a doctor's certificate necessary.'

'What's been the matter?'

I gave a few more discreet hacks. 'I've had this cough and I've been very anaemic and pulled down.'

The clerk studied me carefully and I prayed that my make-up had not smudged.

'Are you feeling all right now?' he asked after a few moments scrutiny.

'I'm feeling better,' I replied in a listless voice.

'Um. . . I must say, you are looking very pale. Well, be sure to ring up if you are away again in future. I'll excuse you this time. And,' he went on, giving me a fatherly smile, 'try to pick up during the holidays. The next term will be your last, and you'll want to make the very best of it, I'm sure. Mr Sturges was speaking about you in here the other day and saying that your work was promising and had shown marked improvement of late.'

'What?' I exclaimed in surprise, for it was plain to me that Mr Sturges must have been speaking about someone else.

'Yes, that's what he said,' and the clerk wagged a finger at me. 'We keep an eye on you even though some of you may think we don't.'

I spent the rest of the morning crouched over my drawing board, astride a 'donkey', trying to make the consumptive looking female model somewhat more attractive. It was not going to be possible, I thought uneasily, to absent myself from the college in future. If I did, there was every chance now that I would be discovered and my grant terminated, and that grant money was exceedingly useful to me. I started violently as Mr Sturges bent over my shoulder and told me to get up. He sat himself down on the donkey and gave a cursory glance at my drawing, a disapproving one.

'Nevah,' he drawled loudly, 'alter the model, not while you are a student. Why have you fattened her up? She's certainly not so well padded as all that, is she?' And with his pencil he swiftly drew an angular and remarkably life-like figure beside mine. Then he turned round. 'What is your name?' he asked.

'Miss Farre.'

'How long have you been here?'

'This is my fifth term.'

'That's odd. I can't remember seeing you here before. Turn over your paper and start again. Don't try and beautify; you are here to draw what you see.'

As far as my art went, I knew exactly in what category I came, and the knowledge did not thrill me. Elderly people would look at my paintings and give vent to such exclamations as, 'How nice!' 'What a charming painting – I can't think why more artists don't stick to subjects like old ivy-covered barns and cows grazing in meadows instead of turning out this hideous modern stuff,' and 'One thing I like about your paintings is that you can always tell the difference between a cat and a cuttlefish in them, which is more than you can with a lot of painting these days.'

I would growl inwardly at these comments, and I sometimes felt that if one more well-meaning individual should say that a painting of mine was nice or charming I would go berserk. Yet I knew that it was useless for me to try anything more adventurous; I had made the attempt and failed. Before leaving the art college I had had several of my paintings exhibited at the more conservative galleries. But on the occasions I had taken my more inspired work to the more go-ahead galleries for inspection each painting in turn had been rejected. Nor could I fool myself that the directors had been anything but right in refusing them. Sadly I laid aside my 'Symphony of Outer Space' – a riot of silvery blues and greys – and started to dab away again, in my spare time, at old English barns and cows grazing in meadows. This was the artistic niche, apparently, to which I was fated; I could either stay there or get out. I chose the latter course without any regrets, for there is nothing more galling, to my way of thinking, than to foster throughout a lifetime one's own mediocre talents. Nevertheless, I was thankful for having received a painting grant and did not cease to silently thank the authorities for it. The grant gave me over a year's freedom in which I lived just the kind of life I wanted to, and during that time I did a good deal of writing and filled several exercise books with notes. Perhaps if I had worked harder at my secondary talent I might one day have got as far as joining the dear old ducks in the Royal Academy who religiously stick to painting society lovelies, pet pekes, and pretty landscapes, and mouth at anything 'modern' as being decadent and tripe into the bargain, though some of their pekes and lovelies look remarkably decadent to me.

During the final week before the start of the lengthy summer holidays – two months of absolute freedom without a care in the world – I was very busy indeed putting in a little overtime at the school. During my spare hours I would set out to visit the galleries clad in one-strap sandals, slacks and a sweatshirt, the latest fashion in students' wear at the time.

I paid many visits to the Tate to look at Blake's paintings, and afterwards I would saunter slowly along the Embankment, across Trafalgar Square, and into the National Portrait Gallery. I would ask one of the attendants to accompany me to the room where undisplayed portraits are hung on large wooden panels, and request him to slide out the one on which hangs a portrait of George Borrow, painted by his brother when Borrow was twenty-one. Next, I would step upstairs to pay my respects to the Brontes, bypassing the portraits of Belloc and Chesterton, those two mutual backslappers whom I number among my unfavourite authors, and go on to have a look at the Lelys and other paintings by seventeenth-century artists.

At the weekend I travelled out to Mitcham to visit some friends of Jai's, housebound Gypsies who lived near the common. The only time they left town, they told me, was during the hop-picking season in Kent. Then they set off in hired trailers to do a stint in the fields.

The following week the school broke up, for which I was duly thankful. Already I was missing Jai, the country and open-air life and could hardly wait to get back. And yet I knew that I would miss the cultural side of London after I returned. I was finding it increasingly difficult to satisfy both heart and mind.

I cleared out my locker, packed away my slacks and sandals, and took the train back to Stratford. The town seemed to be as full of bustling crowds as London. The 'season' was now at its height, a rather different season to that which was going on in the outlying areas.

Jai was still out working when I arrived back, and the trailer was locked. I dumped down my valise, gave the dog a pat, and went to see

Mrs Fennet, who had taken a day off from field work to go bikkining.

'Any news since I've been away?' I asked.

'I can't think of anything special that's happened. Things seem to be going on much the same as usual. I got rid of all my flowers this morning and some pegs as well. Thurzie and Isidor seem to be settling down all right – at least I ain't heard of any sounds of fighting coming from their trailer so far. Now I think of it, Jai mentioned to me the other day that he'd put up a shelf in your trailer for your books.'

'That'll be useful,' I said.

'Oh, there is one bit of good news – they've left.' She pointed to the other side of the field. 'Baby and all.'

'Why, so they have.' Tent, man, woman and their brood had all gone. 'Did you ask them where they were heading for?' I enquired.

'I didn't ask them and they didn't mention where they was going. All I hope is, we don't meet up with them again at the next farm. We're leaving tomorrow – all of us. Picking's over here; finished today. And we're all going on to separate farms. Jai says he's found a new place where you're both going to, north of Stratford, quite small, so he says, and it's likely you'll be the only travellers there.'

The thought of being on our own for a while pleased me. No sooner had he returned than Jai confirmed this information. We were going to a small fruit farm he had heard about from a local worker. The farmer had not taken on travellers before, and he only wanted two outside hands for an orchard of early plums.

'Good, that's fine,' I said, and started to prepare supper.

As I stood at the window, scraping carrots and peeling potatoes, and looking out every so often at the differing shades of green of trees and grass which made up the view, I thought of the changes that my life had undergone during the year, changes that would, I knew, affect me to my dying day. And the stream of time was running faster than the placid surface of the waters indicated. Soon, sooner than I cared, I would be brought face to face with a decision which I was still no nearer to solving than I had been when it first presented itself to me. In order to turn my thoughts from it once again, I cast my mind back to the year before, and relived some of the incidents and happy memories over again.

That year, when I was not attending the art school, I had travelled with the Boswells and another Gypsy family in horse-drawn wagons. This leisurely way of travelling I found very pleasant, particularly in fine weather. The countryside passed slowly before my eyes to the accompaniment of the clip clop of hooves. The bare winter hedgerows had become green and then blossomed with white and pink may flowers. The green deepened, wild roses climbed over the hedgerows. And then trees and bushes became tinged with yellow and russet, and the reds and orange of hips and haws. When autumn came the hedges were covered with Old Man's Beard which was blown away across the fields by the wind. And then the bare branches and withered leaves were rimed with the first frost.

Much as I had enjoyed this way of travel, I prefer the modern trailer every time. From the woman's point of view it is the gas stove which makes such a difference – not having to get a fire going on a cold, wet morning. Moreover, the trailers are more spacious than the wagons and a good deal easier to keep clean. They have a sink, toilet and large water container, and an extra cupboard for brooms and dustpans, all separate from the living room. I am all for a few modern comforts where the travelling life is concerned, for, even at its best, the life is hard enough.

I found that my work was to be increased somewhat, for before my return Jai had acquired a pet dog, a smooth-haired, black-and-white terrier called Betty. And as we ate supper that evening in the trailer, he talked of getting a pure-bred Alsatian. This did not worry me in spite of the extra work entailed. The more animals, the better, so far as I was concerned. 'Go ahead and get one,' I said.

No sooner had we arrived at the next farm and unhitched the trailer, than Jai drove off in the brake to go and look at a likely animal he had heard about, while I made up an extra quantity of food for the dogs' afternoon feed in anticipation of a possible extra and large mouth.

Before long, Jai was back again with a fine adolescent Alsatian and a big orange box to act as a temporary kennel. He did not feel that Tom would welcome the newcomer under the trailer for a day or two, this having been his own private domain up to now. The young dog was leashed to a plum tree and the orange box placed by the trunk. No sooner did he find himself secured then he started to howl and whine, and Tom's coat bristled along the back as he snarled at his new companion in a passion of fury. Not to be outdone, Betty, who was in the trailer, leapt from one piece of furniture to another and peered intently through the window at the unhappy animal outside, all the while emitting ferocious barks. To add to the considerable din, every so often Jai would curse the lot of them to kingdom come. When his threats and curses proved useless, he took hold of a leather strap and swung it upwards, whereupon Tom would bolt under the trailer or, if he had not been quick enough, there would be a sharp howl of pain followed by a minute's comparative quiet. Then there would come a low growl of fury and jealousy from under the trailer, or a whine of sheer misery from the orange box, which would evoke a shrill bark from Betty and off they would all go again.

'Don't beat them, Jai!' I kept repeating. 'They'll quieten down soon. They can't keep it up much longer.'

'Oh, they'll keep it up till morning if they think they can, but I'm taking care they don't.'

I went and turned on the portable radio, then stepped outside again into the warm evening air. The dulcet sounds of a palm-court orchestra drifted from the trailer, along with a few staccato barks for accompaniment.

'I like that music,' said Jai, laying down the strap he had been brandishing over the Alsatian. 'I could listen to it for a half a day at a stretch, along with a bit of jazz to liven thing up. That's one thing I'll always be sorry about – not being able to play an instrument, not even a mouth organ.'

I removed the lid from the cook-pot and gave the contents a stir. 'It's nice having the place to ourselves,' I said.

'Yes, it makes a change.'

We ate the stew by the fire, the smoke keeping the flies and midges off. Afterwards Jai gathered some ripe plums and we ate those. The pickers are quite at liberty to take what fruit they want for their own needs, though this does not mean, of course, filling a bin and doing a little jam-making on one's own behalf.

Jai closed his eyes as a thick gust of smoke blew over him, and then continued to gaze into the fire. Sometimes for hours at a stretch we hardly said a word to one another, but there was never any sense of strain between us. And it would seem to me, as the hours slipped by, each one lived out and fulfilled, with the bond between us becoming stronger each day, that it was now possible I might grow into this wandering life completely – or almost completely – and that we would not have to part. I used to watch Jai attentively when he appeared to be absorbed in his own thoughts or was busy about some job, and sometimes I would catch him watching me. It was as though we were assessing one another and trying to find out the strength of our relationship, for we both knew that if it were to endure I would have to leave the world I came from without regret.

In a way, this should not have been so difficult, for I did not really care for the world I had left and which frequently drew me back again into its orbit; yet a thousand subtle strands bound me tightly to it. I knew that in a lifetime I could never hope to cut them all, but it seemed to me then that it was possible I might sever most of them and so set myself free to live in the world of the travellers and stay in it, and never return to that other less cherished world. At other times I was less optimistic that I would make the break, and the thought would come to me that I was only a brief bird of passage in Jai's life, and he in mine, and that we must inevitably part.

Jai turned to me and broke the silence. 'I've been thinking,' he said. 'If you leave me and go your own way, things will never be the same for me again. I'll get rommerred one day, I don't doubt, and travel the drom as usual. But I'll always be restless, looking for something I can't find, and wanting something I've lost. You'll have put an ache in my heart which wasn't there before and made me dissatisfied with my own life.'

'No!' I protested.

'Yes, that's what you've done for me, Reena,' He took hold of my arm and pulled me towards him. 'Listen. You came from your world and into mine – because it attracted you, gave you something, maybe. All right. Now get this straight. I've never wanted anything from your world; I've always been quite contented with mine. So you're the one who has to do all the adjusting and giving up. I'm sorry, but that's just the way it is. There's no need for you to feel hard done by, the way I see it. We're both happy together, and if you go away for good we'll both be miserable and unsettled for a long while. You've got to learn to pick the big things in life, Reena, and leave the rest. What the hell does your art matter compared with our life together? Give it up – chuck it, and make up your mind once and for all to stay with me. And don't go off on any more solo trips to London. You only come back more undecided than ever.'

'Perhaps I do, but it's not such –'

'Don't give me that again! "It's not such a simple matter to decide, Jai." That's a saying of yours I've heard once too often. What you've got to decide is quite simple. Just say you'll stay with me for keeps and don't change your mind again. Life spoils if you drift, sweetheart.'

I sat staring at the flames, saying nothing. The dogs had stopped barking and the only sounds were the twittering of the linnets in their cage and the chirp of wild birds in the surrounding foliage.

THIRTEEN
Picking

AT THIS FARM we had the working day more or less to ourselves. Occasionally the farmer's wife and a couple of the farm hands would take a few hours off from regular duties to help us with the picking.

When engaged in plum-picking the men usually wear a wide leather belt through which they fix the handle of the basket and so leave both hands free for picking the fruit. Ladders are placed against the tree trunks to enable the workers to climb up into the higher branches and strip the whole tree.

There was nothing I enjoyed more than climbing up into the trees, for here one was in a different world amongst a sea of green leaves, with hardly a foot of square earth to be seen. Jai and I would talk to each other as we worked at neighbouring trees. Sometimes half of Jai's body emerged from out of the treetops, at other times I would see just his head, or an arm stretched out to pick the ripe fruit. Or he might not be visible at all, and only his voice would come to me or the sound of his movements among the branches. Sometimes we worked the same tree together. On the grass lay the wicker baskets and chips filled with fruit, ready to be taken into Stratford or Evesham. As I picked in my leafy domain up in the branches I was ever conscious of the sky and the wind. The wind sometimes blew so strongly that it was necessary to keep one hand clasped round a branch and to pick with the other.

'Jai, what are you doing?' I called out, not having heard a sound from his direction for some while.

'Taking the dogs for a walk,' he called back.

'Taking time off, I imagine. Get busy.'

We returned to the trailer for a snack about noon. It was parked at the far end of the orchard and the roadway ran on the other side of the hedge. As we ate, an occasional passer-by, seeing the trailer roof above the hedge, would push open the gate and come and take a look at our home and camping ground. The dogs set up a furious barking at the approach of these strangers. Thanks to the dogs, various nosey parkers were kept away from our home as we worked in the orchards. No sooner had we finished eating than I started on some mending and Jai tinkered about in the engine of the brake. It is a gorgio fallacy that the traveller spends large portions of his life stretched out in front of the yog, or poaching for game in private woodlands. The traveller works hard for the greater part of the year, and should he ever feel like taking a brief holiday from his labours, then it is a holiday without pay. In fact, holidays in the gorgio sense of the word, are unknown amongst the travelling fraternity.

When we returned to the orchard the sky had turned so dark that it seemed we would have to stop work almost before we had started. I stood under some branches, pulling off the fruit in almost total darkness. Drops of heavy rain fell on the leaves. I climbed a ladder and emerged through the topmost branches of a tall plum tree to gaze at the threatening sky. All around me thin leafy twigs and slender branches tossed like breakers. I stretched forward to grab a fruit, only for it to swing away out of my grasp. My hair kept blowing about my head and into my eyes, so I tied a scarf around my head. Jai was wearing a navy-blue sweater and he looked like a mariner breasting the waves as he leant forward and then back, picking the fruit and placing it in the basket suspended from his waist. When I next glanced in his direction he had disappeared, except for a hand which stretched upwards like that of a drowning man's in supplication to the grey skies. The wind increased, twigs snapped, and ripe fruit fell with gentle thuds upon the grass. Up above, clouds dissolved, reformed, and assumed strange shapes.

'Jai,' I called. 'Where are you, up or down?'

'Here, on the ground. You'd better climb down too. It's going to pelt in a few seconds.'

I descended into the twilight, subterranean world of the trunks and lower branches. Betty, whom I had brought with me that afternoon, was curled up by some chips. She opened her eyes and yawned as rain suddenly started to fall in torrents. I wiped my sticky fingers on the grass, and Jai sat down and lit a cigarette. The wind roared and the leaves fluttered like a thousand wings. A strange, haunting quality had crept into the atmosphere which turned my thoughts from everyday things.

'I wonder if we'll remember each other in a thousand years' time,' I said, speaking my thoughts out aloud.

'Stop thinking so far into the future. It's the present that counts. Be happy now.'

'I am happy now.'

'Good. And remember that you were this time next season, and the year after that if you're still around.'

He stubbed out his cigarette, then leant the full weight of his body on mine. Around us it was as dark as night. We were alone together, away from the rest of the world, from friends and enemies. Even the immediate outer world – the trees, the grass and rain – was as far away as the stars, and it seemed that we were the only beings in existence.

The following day was so hot that I wore my straw hat as I worked. I had sewn ribbons on to it which tied under the chin so that it would not blow off in the wind. Every so often I sucked a ripe plum, or rested for a few minutes on a branch, under a dome of leaves, to cool off. The sky was a clear blue, whitened with great masses of cumuli.

'Let's have some tea,' Jai called.

I jumped down, picked up the thermos lying in the grass, and poured out two mugfuls.

'Another day and we should have finished,' he said.

'And where do we go to next?' I asked.

'Nowhere for a while; that is, we stick around here. We'll lay off work for a bit, at least as far as picking's concerned. I want to see if I can find some more brasses. You take the kipsie and go bikkining. We'd better get some flowers made up this evening. I've got some sticks stored away in a box somewhere.'

'Have you asked the farmer if we can stay here until we move on for hop-picking?'

'Yes. He said that would be all right. I'll help out on the farm in between my own jobs.'

Just before we finished work that day in the orchards we heard the dogs starting to bark. When we got back to the trailer there was Fish-fry sitting between the two large animals who were rising up on their hind legs and straining against the leashes in an endeavour to get a mouthful of him. But Fish-fry leant back calmly on an elbow and sucked a plum.

'Well, this is a surprise,' I said. 'I didn't expect to see you.'

'Why not?' he asked. 'It might as well be me as anybody else. D'you mind if I pitch here one night? I'll rig up a tan o' sorts.'

So far as we were concerned, he was welcome to stay. It was unlikely the farmer or any of the hands would come down to the camping ground at this hour.

'When I saw this trailer I knew you was here,' he said to me.

'How was that?' I asked.

'I'd only been in the Vale a short while when I was told that a gorgio girl called Reena, who'd been putting up with a family called Boswell, had gone off with a Romany called Jai,' and Fish-fry gave a wink. 'I first heard that piece o' news from a couple of young travellers called Lisha and Gilbert who was working on the same farm as me. They said you had spent a night in their wagon on the way up.'

'That's right. I did.'

'They was ever so interested when someone told them you'd gone off with this young man. Quite a lot of people are talking about you two.'

'Are they now?' said Jai. 'Well, it's nice to know they've got some news to keep their tongues busy.'

'Yes, they're all keen to know how the pair of you are getting on.'

'We're getting on all right, thanks,' said Jai.

'Good, it's pleasant to know that. I don't like to hear of young folks scrapping.'

'But how did you guess I was here when you saw the trailer?' I asked.

'I reckon I've got every trailer and wagon taped; know who's in which and who's shifted to another, and who's sold their old one and bought a new one, and who's had to sell their nice new one and buy an old one instead.'

We laughed. 'Where's Len?' I enquired. 'I thought you two always travelled together.'

'Yes, we usually do, but we've split up for a while. He's not far from here. We'll be meeting up again later in the hop fields. I'll tell you a piece of news you mayn't have heard about. Remember that Pole Sergei, silent chap, who was at the same farm with us? Well, he and Saluki met up again somewhere and now they're travelling together. Even talking of getting hitched proper and renting a room down Aldgate East for the winter.'

'That's certainly news to me,' I said.

'I don't suppose the poor chap gets so much as a word in edgewise with Saluki around, from one week to the next. And if I know her, she'll look after his pay for him. Maybe she'll buy him a new pair of socks as a Christmas present with some of the money he's earned, just to keep him happy.'

'Well, maybe her company will do him good all the same,' I said. 'He looked pretty lonely to me.'

'If it was a case of being lonely and only having the sparrows to talk to, or going with Saluki and having her talking to me, I know what I'd choose. Give me the sparrows every time.'

After supper Fish-fry erected a little bothie from two bent poles and some sacking, and in this flimsy shelter he spent the night. The following morning he cooked himself a breakfast of fried toast and kippers. Then, with a cheerful smile, he bid us goodbye and set off along the road in the direction of Worcester.

FOURTEEN

Hop Harvest

A T THE END OF AUGUST we too moved north-west in the direction of Worcester. Around the towns of Worcester, Bromyard and Ledbury are the biggest hop fields in this part of England. Hundreds more workers join the ranks of the pickers at this season. Some are miners and their wives, who spend a week in the fields and then go on to the seaside for the final week of their annual holidays, others are 'settled' travellers who leave their homes just for the hop harvest and come to the fields in hired trailers. The genuine travellers only comprise about half the workers these days.

Before motoring on to the hop fields, we made a special journey into Worcester where I bought about five pounds' worth of groceries so that I would not have to make journeys into the neighbouring town while picking was in progress. Vegetables, bread, milk and butter could be purchased locally.

Once again we joined up with Thurzie and Isidor, Hiram and Fanny, and we pitched our trailers together at the end of a large field given over entirely to the pickers. Tents, huts, wagons, and trailers were dispersed around the field. Across the road, in the fields opposite, stretched acres of tall, green hops. The pointed towers of the oast houses made landmarks in this district. Mr and Mrs Boswell were down near Ledbury. And at another farm, also near Ledbury, were Deborah and Tarsh.

Before leaving the Vale, Hiram had chopped his brake for a small lorry in which could be stowed bits and pieces of furniture, and these had been placed outside his hatchin-tan; a table, three wooden chairs, a chest-of-drawers, on top of which was a large mirror. Fanny did her hair in front of this mirror every morning. Kept in the lorry when not in use were Lockwood's and Eudocia's bicycle, and that necessity of Gypsy life, a pram which was used on shopping expeditions.

We started picking the hops on the day following our arrival. Work started at eight-thirty. The sun was shining brightly. With any luck, the weather would hold until the hops were gathered. Heavy rain or early frost can halve the yield, and the workers are as keen as the farmers to get the crop in.

We worked from one end of the field steadily forwards, day by day, to the far end. The hops were picked from the bines and placed in cribs – trestles with a piece of canvas across – and each group or family kept to its own crib. When picked, the separated hops are driven to the kilns to be dried out and this process takes about a year. They are then placed in long sacks, called pockets, and sold to the breweries.

The sweet, pungent smell of the hops rose in the air. If only beer tasted like the smell of hops, I thought, what a pleasant drink it would be, for I dislike the taste of this brew, and it always seems something of a come-down to me when the aromatic heads are transformed, along with other ingredients, into the bitter, sickly drink.

'Yes,' said Thurzie, as we worked side by side at a crib and who shared my opinion of beer, 'give me a glass of cider or a cup of mookerimungeri every time. I can't bide the stuff. By the way, has anyone seen that the pails are on?'

We walked over to the 'oven', a square of low bricks which enclosed a fire, over which was set two pails of water on some iron bars. Everyone had their own mug, often a special tea mug which had a looped handle and cover. Thurzie and I poured boiling water from the pails into some kettles and called out that tea was made. There was a tall enamel jug containing about six pints of milk from which you helped yourself. If you wanted sugar you brought your own.

Thurzie took a long gulp of tea then pulled a newly cut bine towards the crib, and once more we set to, pulling the light yellowy-green hopheads from the stalks.

'Oh, stop it, Jai!' I begged. He had sneaked up behind me and tied my ankles together with a length of stripped bine.

'That's to keep you at the crib working,' he said. 'I'll come and untie you at the lunchbreak.'

I kicked the bine loose and continued to separate hops and leaves.

'At that farm over there they've got a mechanical separator,' said Thurzie. 'I reckon that in a few years' time they won't be taking on any more outside labour in these parts – and other parts of the country as well, likely as not.'

She had voiced what I had been thinking before now; that it would not be long before this annual crop would be harvested almost entirely by machine, and another source of employment would have closed to the travellers forever.

After picking was over for the day, some of the men went off to the pubs directly they had eaten while the women enjoyed a spell of idleness. Two farm workers had brought some planks down to the field and these were laid out to form a clog-dancing pitch. Eudocia and Lockwood, along with other children, started to kick up their heels on the planks, while a Gypsy youth played the accordion.

Jai and I had our trailer to ourselves. I drew the blinds and got out my drawing materials, then sat down to do a little sketching, using Jai as a model. He was never particularly helpful during these short sessions in which he allowed me to draw him, but then amateur models seldom are. Nevertheless, they are usually more rewarding to the artist than the professional variety one gets in the art schools.

He stretched his long, graceful body on the bunk and laid me to hurry up. 'Can I smoke?' he asked, when he had been lying there for some thirty seconds.

'No,' I answered.

'Hell! I'm going to.'

I sighed and put down my pencil while he extricated a packet of cigarettes and lighter from his jacket hanging on the door. Then he took up his reclining position again. 'Would you mind crossing your ankles and keeping one arm over your chest as before?' I asked.

'I'm not crossing anything till I've finished this cigarette.'

'Ye gods! Patience is a virtue.' Once more I laid down my pencil.

'You're telling me. . . I'm tired out keeping this pose. You've got five more minutes and then I'm getting up.'

'Would you put a cushion under your head. I can't see enough of your face the way you are.'

He groaned, but did as I requested.

After a few brief minutes, during which I scribbled away like one possessed, he got up and went to the kitchen. While he was out, I taped the drawing to a wall.

'I wonder what the others will think when they see this sketch,' I said when he came in. 'It's not too bad, all things considered. Looks nice up there. I think I'll leave it.'

'Jumping snakes! Don't tell me you've been and stuck that drawing on the wall. You know, Reena,' he said, rising like a fish to my little joke, 'there are times when you scare me. I mean it. If anyone came in and saw that drawing of me in the nude I'd never live it down to the end of my life.'

'Wouldn't you? Careful how you pull it off the wall. I don't want it torn. I'm rather pleased with it.'

'Well, keep it stowed away in the somewhere, under cover.'

The strains of the accordion floated down the field.

'I wish that chap would try and hit the right note occasionally,' I said.

'Oh, he's not so bad. He's got a good sense of rhythm, and that's the main thing.'

He pulled open a drawer and took out his comb and started to draw it through his hair. 'Reena, would you tong my hair for me this evening, please? I want some of the slack taken up. It kept getting into my eyes today as I worked.'

'Yes, certainly. And I'll cut some off too, if you like.'

'No, thanks. I don't trust you with the scissors. Just put in an extra wave or two with the tongs.'

I brought out the burner and placed the tongs over it. His hair was naturally wavy, but he liked to have the waves reinforced a little and a few more added.

'Might I try out a new style?' I asked. 'Part the hair in the centre and sweep it forward over the brows.'

'Just keep it the way it is. That's what I meant about you and the scissors – given half a chance you'd have me clipped like one of those French poodles.'

'Very well, I'll try to restrain my artistic impulse.'

'And after you've made a good job of my head, let's have a chapter of the book. I like you reading out to me in the evenings. Leave off a moment; I'll fetch it.'

'Oh, Jai!' I begged. 'Can't you keep still for one minute?'

He walked over to the bookshelf he had rigged up, and pulled out the cowboy paperback from between a copy of Wuthering Heights and a volume of Traherne's poetry.

'It was a good idea of yours to turn down the top of the page like this so as to remember the place. What did you call it?'

'Dog-earing,' I replied. 'Now please sit down and give me a clear ten minutes to work on your head.'

I picked up the heated tongs and closed them on a portion of hair for

a few seconds. He used a liberal quantity of oil on his hair and the heat
from the tongs brought out the scent, so that the living room soon smelt
like some heavily perfumed oriental boudoir.

'Finished?' he asked presently.

'Yes, I suppose so.'

He looked at himself in the mirror. 'Yes, that will do. Now let's have
half an hour of blood and thunder.'

I sat down on the couch and started to read. Jai stretched out and laid
his head on my lap.

'I never bothered to learn to read even though I had the chance once,'
he said, interrupting the narrative. 'Maybe that shocks a learned little
cuss like you.'

'I'm not so easily shocked,' I said.

Nevertheless, I was getting bored with reading out this cowboy
melodrama and our reading sessions were becoming more and more of
a chore.

He looked up at me as though he had sensed something of my feelings
and said, 'I'm not really so interested in the story either. It's just that I
like you reading out to me like this. After we've finished this book we
could start on one of those classics, as you call them, up on the shelf. It's
all the same to me.'

It's all the same to me. . . A casual remark of his would sometimes
underline the impossibility of our living together always; useless and
dangerous to try, for both our lives might be wrecked in the effort. And
it was for me to make the break. As I laid the book down, I thought:
September – I've got three more months till the end of the year.

The hop-picking continued unbroken by storms. Tractors roared
down the lanes and each day the workers advanced steadily across the
fields. We had stripped one field completely of bines, and only the poles
and the wires were left standing. An atmosphere of cheerfulness and
goodwill pervaded the fields, almost a holiday atmosphere. Between the
green lanes the workers cut down the bines and stood long hours at the
cribs. Scrub my fingers hard as I did in the evenings, they nevertheless

retained a permanent green tinge which had worked its way under the cuticles. My arms, face, and legs, like everybody else's, were a deep brown and this tan disguised somewhat the sorry state of my hands. Gypsies in their open carts rattled down to the pubs in the evening and not all of them came back sober. In our tin box were now some two hundred bars, most of them in five-pound notes.

Although our weekly earnings amounted to what many persons would consider little enough, yet during this time and most of the other periods when I lived the traveller's life, I was seldom at all short of money. I had everything I wanted so far as the material side of life was concerned and money was never a problem. In contrast, when I worked in London, no matter what I was earning, I was always short of cash, often acutely so. By the time I had paid my rent, food, fuel, and travelling expenses I was lucky if I had ten shillings left over from my pay-packet. I got a lot of fun and pleasure earning my living in the fields and hawking, but no fun or pleasure whatsoever from the work I did in town; it was slave labour with a vengeance.

One mid-morning I was returning from the hop fields and pushed open the gate leading into the field where the trailers and wagons were parked, when there came the sound of trotting hooves and the rattle of a trap and presently my eardrums were rent by a loud screech: 'Reena!'

I did not have to turn round to find out who had emitted this cry which resembled that of a husky corncrake. The trap was packed tight with travellers who sat with their legs dangling over the sides. Saluki Waine jumped down with a large bundle under one arm, and she was followed by the Pole.

'Thanks for the lift,' she called to the Gypsy who was holding the reins, and the cart rattled off down the road.

Jai and Hiram had been following on behind me, each carrying a bucket of water. 'Who on earth's that?' Jai asked, nodding at Saluki's scarecrow figure.

'She's called Saluki Waine,' I said in a low voice.

The newcomers adjusted the bundles under their arms and walked along beside us, Saluki chattering without a pause all the way.

'Ah, there's the huts,' she said. 'I can spot an empty one from here. We were at the Labour Exchange in Worcester yesterday and they told us this farm needed more workers. We got two lifts here which brought us right to the front door, as you might say. The first was in the back of a coal lorry and second in that trap. I've got some news for you, Reena – you'd never guess! And I know all about you and your goings on. Which of these two young Romanies here is the one you're living with?'

'Him,' I said, indicating Jai.

'Good for you. Always pick the best looking, that's what I say. It makes such a difference when you wake up first thing in the morning to have a good looking chap lying beside you. Kind of starts the day right.'

The expression on Hiram's face was none too sunny after her tactless remark, but Saluki was quite unaware of any coolness towards her from his direction. 'Now for my news. It's about Setter and me. I don't call him Sergei any more. We're two dogs together now. We've been going steady for quite a while and we're thinking of settling down and getting hitched in a registry office. It's difficult to see myself married after all these years. Still, at my age it's not such a bad idea, and Setter doesn't think so either. There's a bit of difference in our ages; I'm getting on for fifty-six and he says he's thirty-one. Still, I never did agree with the man being the older of the two.'

'I hope things work out all right for you both,' I said.

'I'm sure they will. Which is the trailer you're living in?'

I pointed it out to her, and as I did so I saw Jai's mouth set.

'I'll come over and see you, Reena, when we've got settled in the hut. If you could spare a few odds and ends of food – some bread, butter, a bit of cheese, perhaps, some salt and a little tea. . . Oh, and we lost our fork at the last farm. If you have one to spare maybe you'd lend it to us just while we're here. I'll try and get into Worcester next Saturday and buy another.'

She pointed to Setter, with a look of satisfaction on her face. 'Notice the difference in him since you last saw him, Reena?'

Frankly, I couldn't, but I took care not to say so.

'It's all due to me, since I've been feeding him up on chips and baked beans. It's wonderful what love can do for a man.

'Well, see you later.'

When the pair were out of earshot Jai said to me, 'She's not putting one toe in the trailer. And you're not going to lend, give, or let her pinch any darned thing.'

'It's going to be a bit awkward, then, when she comes over,' I said.

To my relief, Saluki visited a wagon nearer the hutments after she got unpacked, and managed to extract what she wanted.

But she often came over to us for a gossip, and on these occasions Jai would lie silently on the bunk or go and talk to the others. Nobody, except for myself, paid any attention to her when she came down our end, though Thurzie and the rest of our group would be pleasant enough should she chat with us in the hop fields. The Gypsies always try to keep the mumper fraternity away from the wagons and trailers, owing to their well-founded reputation for begging and pilfering. Fanny, who was very prejudiced against them, lectured me on their many foibles and vices. She told me that when she was a chie, her mother had been indicted by the police for a theft committed by a mumper woman. 'And I've known that happen many a time to others outside my family. Just tell her to keep off, Reena, and the same with that Pole she's got with her. I don't like the look of him at all.'

Fanny often wore a brooding, faraway expression and would sit silently by the fire, smoking a clay pipe, without ever blinking her large hazel eyes. She had been born in a wagon up in the Black Mountains. There was something hieratic about her, as though she had knowledge of the arcana which had been passed down through countless generations from one to another of her race. There was a reserve about her too, and Thurzie had once admitted to me that even she was not always able to penetrate it. Hiram had been passionately in love with Fanny, and he still was. When he was courting her – and he was by no means the only racklo in pursuit, so I gathered, for she seemed to hold a fascination for men – he took the unusual course of hiring a trailer and following her drom. Her parents and the Boswells had been very much against the match, but eventually Hiram had managed to persuade Fanny to go off with him. In order to bind her to him more closely, he had gone to the trouble of getting married in a registry office, no easy task, for neither could produce birth certificates. But a Methodist minister had come to their aid and the ceremony had gone through with him acting as a witness. Hiram often bought his wife expensive jewellery with any spare cash he had, and this would annoy Mrs Kizer and Deborah when they heard about it, for Fanny already had a large collection of gold jewellery and a velvet-lined box to keep it in, another present from Hiram. Fanny accepted these gifts with pleasure and refused to chop them even when money was scarce.

'Now just remember what I've told you about that warfedo crowd o' mumpers,' Fanny bid me. 'Jai,' she called, 'you git telling her about that crowd of sleevers otherwise we'll be having them all around here and I couldn't abide that.'

'I've told her,' he said.

'Da!' Fanny knocked out her pipe against the table. 'Where'll you be pitching this winter, or haven't you decided yet?' she asked Jai, changing the subject.

'I'm thinking of going Bristol way and starting a chop-mart for brakes and cars. I've got a friend who'll come in with me.'

'Why don't you and Reena come to North Wales with us, close by Dolgelly? Last winter we hatchin-tanned the whole winter in a woodyard and paid half a bar's rent a week. The man who owns the place said he'd be willing to take two trailers next year for only seven shillings each. I've asked Thurzie if she'd like to pitch alongside us, but she says she and Isidor want to pitch by themselves.'

'What sort of work can you get round those parts?' Jai asked.

'There's plenty of work going in logs and scrap iron and the hawking's not bad at all.'

'I'll think about it,' said Jai. 'I like Bristol but maybe Dolgelly will do for a change.'

'I think Bristol's a horrible town,' said Thurzie, coming up. 'I been down there once and I wouldn't go and hatchin-tan there for the whole winter, not for anything. If we didn't head north most winters, then I'd go to the Forest; but you'd never catch me going to that nasty, ugly old place except for a day's shopping.'

'If you decide to come, Jai,' said Fanny, filling her pipe, 'then Reena could write a letter to this man who owns the yard and tell him we'll be arriving in about two weeks, after the hops are picked. I tell you, once you've headed up North Wales you'll never go South again. And you'll have good company round about for the winter. Why not say now that you'll come along?'

Jai thought for a moment, looked at me, then said, 'Misto, we'll come.'

Just then Lockwood, who had been whittling a peg, with one eye on his parents' dog, sprang to his feet. 'Cah!' he exclaimed. 'Look what him's caught, a sho-sho. I didn't think there was hardly any o' them left. I thought that they'd all died from that disease that makes their eyes pop out of their heads. Kooshti jukel, come here!' And he sped after the lurcher who did not appear to be in a hurry to give up its catch.

'Him's a real fine jukel,' said Fanny. 'One of the best we've ever had.'

Lockwood managed to get an arm round the big black animal's neck and to extract the rabbit.

'Bring that sho-sho here, Lockwood,' said Fanny. 'I want to see that it's not diseased afore I put it in the stew pot.'

Fanny went carefully over the rabbit and then, to the general satisfaction of everybody, pronounced it fit eating. Hiram skinned it and removed the entrails, and the dog was given a piece of bread-and-dripping as a reward for its unwitting labours on behalf of the family larder. Dogs are never given rabbit to eat as the small bones splinter easily and may set up internal injuries or stick fast in the gullet.

Lockwood nailed the rabbit skin on to a piece of board and rubbed salt into the raw side. But after two days he became bored with the curing

process and threw the skin away. Rabbit fur is practically useless and is
seldom used, as the hair moults like a thistle-puff. However, Lockwood
and several other boys, who had been inspired by the lurcher's enterprise,
asked the farmer if they might catch moles in an adjacent field which
was scattered with small earthen hillocks. Permission granted, the boys
got up early one morning and set out with spades to dig in the field. At
breakfast, Lockwood appeared beaming and with two dead moles in
his hands. He skinned the little beasts carefully, tacked the skins on to
the board, and went to the trouble to rub in fresh salt each day until
they were properly cured. When he had collected enough skins, Fanny
was going to make them up into a waistcoat for him. The latest catch
brought his total up to twenty, but it takes at least forty skins to make a
small moleskin waistcoat.

On Sunday we were given the morning off from work. A party of
Salvationists came to the field, one of the men carrying a full-sized
accordion. There was hymn singing, prayers, and a short address for
anyone who cared to join in and listen. At the sounds of the accordion,
the children raced towards the group and joined loudly in the singing.
Thurzie and I made some tea for the party which they drank before
going on to another farm.

This simple outdoor service provoked a diatribe against the Protestant
and Free Churches from the usually silent Pole, who was a Catholic. He
had been walking moodily up and down on the edge of the crowd, and
no sooner had the Salvationists left than he started his abusive talk.

'Shut up!' somebody said.

'Just remember,' I cut in, 'that it was Protestant Britain who
accepted you and hundreds and thousands of other refugees, and saved
Christianity from Fascist and Nazi barbarism.'

He walked off with a scowl on his face.

The children had been given coloured postcards of Bible scenes and
these were passed round admiringly from hand to hand.

That same afternoon we were back again in the hop fields. Jai and I worked together at a crib. When I worked with Thurzie, and Jai along with Hiram, we would 'halve' the amount picked. When the farmhand weighed the pile and it came to, say, six bushels, then that was three each. It was quite a fair way of reckoning as Thurzie and I picked at about the same speed, as did the other two. Eudocia and Lockwood also put in a little spasmodic work. Unlike so many of the travellers' children who would often put in a full day, Fanny and Hiram seemed quite unconcerned as to whether their two worked at all.

I felt among the leaves for the delicate pale green heads. Most days, at the rate paid this season, Jai and I managed to make about three pounds; sometimes a little more, sometimes a little less.

'Two and a half bushels,' said the farmhand. The hops were put into sacks ready to be taken off to the kiln.

'I'll leave you now,' I said to Jai, shaking the pollen off my clothes, 'and go and get supper ready.'

Fanny already had the fire going and her cook-pot was hanging from the crane. She was lying stretched out like a somnolent cat, a wooden spoon in one hand with which she occasionally stirred the stew.

'I feel as if I'd been making love half the afternoon. This warm weather always makes me feel like that,' she said, and gave the contents of the cauldron another stir. There was a big pile of early mushrooms beside her.

'I'll take some of these, if you don't mind,' I said. 'They'll liven up the carrots and potatoes.'

'Help yourself, take what you want. I wish that jukel would catch another sho-sho. Mushrooms and sho-sho go well together.' She yawned. 'I'm not doing much cooking this evening. When the vegetables have softened up I'm opening a tin of steak and putting that in.'

'Good idea. I think I'll do the same.'

'One of the mumper children in the huts has been and swallowed some deadly nightshade berries,' said Fanny. 'Luckily someone spotted him putting them into his mouth. His Ma held him upside down and someone else thumped his back and he spewed up the lot. Them mumpers never seem to teach their chavvies the very first simplest things. Anyway, I reckon that chal's learn his lesson now.'

She got up slowly and went over to the mirror which was set on the chest of drawers. She undid her plaits, combed out her hair and then replaited it.

'How old are you, Fanny?' I asked idly, opening a tin.

'Twenty-eight or roundabouts. I don't suppose I'll live to reach sixty.'

'Why not? You look healthy enough to me.'

'I was very ill as a young girl,' she said. 'At one time Ma and Daddus didn't think I was going to pull through. I woke up one morning to find myself covered all over with a rash and my head throbbing with fever. It was early spring and we had pitched in a quiet little place by Cardigan Bay. I stayed in the tan, lying on a camp bed Daddus had bought cheap from some holidaymakers the summer before. About the third day after I'd been taken ill I lay on the bed thinking I wasn't going to live much longer. Everyone was out except for the jukels, and they were tied up. So I thought I must be seeing things when something like a small dog came walking in through the door of the tan. It was dark and it had long whiskers and its coat was wet from swimming. Daddus said later it must have been a sea otter. After it had taken a good look around, it went out again and I raised myself up on an elbow to see where it went. It walked straight down the grass towards the sea where the waves were lapping on a little beach. Straight into the waves it went, and swam off.

'I don't know why it was, but after that I somehow knew I was going to get better. When Ma got back from hawking, I told her about my visitor, and she said, 'That otter came specially to see you and tell you to get better, Fan.' 'Yes. I believe you, Ma,' I said, 'I reckon that's why he came.' And that very same evening I was sitting up in bed drinking cups of mookery, as chirpy as a lark.'

FIFTEEN

The Woodyard

THE HOP-PICKING SEASON lasts about a month. We moved three times in all, from one farm on to the next. The wind began to have an edge to it and the first traces of Old Man's Beard appeared on the hedgerows. Trailers and wagons started to leave the fields as the last of the bines were stripped and the hops stored away in the kilns. Some Gypsies made for winter quarters while others set off on their winter circuit if the family travelled throughout the year. Travelling is particularly arduous during the winter months when fields are muddy and the weather bitterly cold, and when the roads have a coating of ice on them. But whatever the weather, hatchin-tanned in winter quarters or out on the drom, throughout the year the men trade goods and barter and the women hawk.

I was glad that Jai and I were heading for North Wales as the idea of Bristol had not appealed to me at all. We set off early one morning past the bare hop fields. We travelled slowly to give the Boswells' horse-drawn wagon a chance to catch up with us at the evening camping ground. At the start of each day the four trailers – Hiram's, Tarsh's, Isidor's, and Jai's – would be driven to the next hatchin-tan and the old couple would follow behind at their leisure. We did not always manage to pitch together at the same spot. Most often we split up for the night, having agreed where to meet up the following day. It took the Boswells the best part of a day to reach the next stopping place, whereas the trailers could often get there in an hour. So we would make several halts en route, go marketing, hawk, or just rest up for a while and talk. Unfortunately, old Dan Boswell had not learnt to drive a car or brake, otherwise Hiram or Tarsh would have changed places with him some days and taken the wagon up and down the steep hill country we were traversing. Some of this country is very difficult going for wagons, a strain for both horses and drivers.

Two evenings before reaching our last hatchin-tan, Thurzie and Isidor announced, while we were seated round the yog, that they had decided not to come any further with us but to continue next day in the direction of Aberdovey, a town further to the south. It was clear that the young couple wanted to strike off on their own for a while, even though Thurzie knew for certain now that she was expecting her first child. They promised to come up in their trailer and join us over Christmas.

The old couple's winter pitch was a small woodyard behind an inn which lay a few miles north of ours.

Our own winter quarters, which we were to share with Fanny and Hiram, were set among the Welsh hills and were approached by a gravelled drive. Half way down the drive were the owner's bungalow and some outbuildings, and at the end was the woodyard – a square of land entirely enclosed by a wooden plank wall. At one side of the yard was a rough open-walled shanty under which was stacked timber, trestles, and a variety of saws and axes. The two trailers were parked alongside one of the walls, and the brake and lorry could just be squeezed into the shanty. Only the tops of the trailers could be seen from outside the enclosure, and our privacy was ensured. But few people ever came up this way to trouble us and we were able to lead our own lives in peace and quiet. Outside the yard were meadows and hills and a double row of tall beech trees which wound their way up and around the hills into the horizon. When the winter gales sprang up the branches would creak and knock against each other, and sometimes there would be a sharp crack as one broke off and came hurtling down. At the entrance to the yard was an aluminium rainwater butt and a tap which supplied water from the mains. This was a yard, in fact, well fitted up for Gypsy families.

No sooner had we arrived than furniture was placed outside and the cranes pushed into the ground.

About five days on Fanny and I went out hawking with our baskets filled with wares and the men would put in several hours each day chopping and sawing logs. An unfortunate event occurred soon after our arrival. The school inspector turned up unexpectedly and told Hiram and Fanny that unless the children attended classes regularly they would be up before the courts. Lockwood and Eudocia loathed every minute spent at the local school, and it was extraordinary what those two healthy children managed to contract during the winter in the way of colds, coughs and other ailments which kept them away from the prison house for days at a stretch.

The weeks passed. Golden beech leaves strewed the yard.

I made another brief visit to London, sold off some clothes and other belongings to various students and informed the art school authorities that I would not be completing the term and that therefore I would be giving up my grant. There was a rumpus, and I was told I had wasted Government money and the time of the teaching staff. But I did not believe the money had been wasted and I felt certain that one day I would put what I had learned and absorbed at the school to good use. I returned to Wales via Stratford, having made this detour in order to collect my mail at the Post Office. I had meant to read it during the latter half of my journey on to Wales, write replies to my correspondents en route, then tear up their letters and dispose of them out of the window. I was not going to risk my mail being burnt, unread, again. But I got talking to another passenger for the best part of the journey and forgot to carry out my plan. So when the train pulled up at the small station where I alighted, I stuffed the packet of mail in the bottom of my rucksack, intending to read it some time when Jai was out and I had the trailer to myself.

When I returned, I unpacked a few things from the top of the rucksack, handed Jai a new scarf I had bought for him in town, and pushed the rucksack away in the bottom of the wardrobe.

The following days were frosty and fine. Fanny and I spent long hours hawking and marketing. Sometimes I remembered the mail lying at the bottom of the wardrobe, but whenever I did there was always someone around in the trailer and so I left it unread. However, I did not worry about it; my various correspondents were used to receiving my replies somewhat tardily.

'Since I've lived with you, I can't think of any period of time – over half an hour or so – that I've been alone,' I remarked to Jai one evening as we ate our supper in the trailer, with the wind whistling outside.

'So what? The traveller doesn't want to be alone. This is a community life. If I had to admit to one thing I'm scared of it would be finding myself alone one day. That's every traveller's secret fear. I wasn't really enjoying myself when we met up, living by myself in the trailer, even though I was mixing with people all day long.'

In spite of the cold weather, we often ate out of doors. I would sit muffled up in an old coat with a scarf around my neck and one numb hand in a pocket whilst with the other I spooned up mouthfuls of congealing, tepid stew. But there was always plenty of hot tea to drink, to thaw out and take away the taste of solidified grease.

The Gypsies seem to feel the cold very little, yet they enjoy sitting in stifling wagons which make one gasp longingly for a breath of icy air. The heat in the timber wagons when the stove has been roaring away all day is often well past the state termed a real good fug. Windows are opened just a crack to allow the smallest possible amount of air to enter and prevent the inmates being asphyxiated.

We rose much later in the mornings now, not much earlier than eight or eight-thirty. And after breakfast we often lazed around for an hour or so before starting on the day's work. The big dogs were installed in their winter quarters: two large wooden boxes filled with straw. And I had acquired a wicker basket for Betty with an old cushion in it. Sometimes Jai and Hiram went out together each holding a dog on a leash, and they would return later with something tasty for the pot; a game bird, perhaps, or a hare. Hiram had two ferrets, and these were always muzzled and carefully concealed whenever he took them out of the yard precincts.

During these winter days I was methodically cutting away various ties which bound me to my other life. If the artist in me was to remain largely unfulfilled, then I was ready to pay the price this entailed in exchange for other things I held dearer. I was poised and ready to leave my other life behind.

We ate our Christmas lunch in the Boswells' yard. True to their promise, Thurzie and Isidor had come up in their trailer to join us. The lunch was a gay affair even though it was eaten out of doors in a chill wind with cat ice on the puddles. The barmaid came out with a tray laden with glasses of hot punch, a gift from the landlord.

One frosty day in January when the sky was a clear, sharp blue, I found that I had the afternoon to myself, rather surprisingly.

About half a mile from the woodyard was a big house set in a park. During the winter months it was untenanted, so I had been told, the only person around being the caretaker who lived in one of the cottages on the estate. I decided to climb over the wall and have a look at the place.

The long, grey house was surrounded by clipped hedges, terraces, gravelled paths, ponds strewn with dead leaves, lawns and walks under arbours of curved branches which had been trained to these graceful shapes, no doubt, by generations of gardeners. I sat down in a little summerhouse, opposite which was a bright green hedge of some everlasting greenery. That hedge in the wintry English scene looked somewhat out of place and foreign to me, and I had the certain feeling that in some period of my life I had seen it, or another very similar, before. Then a bird, uttering a sharp cry, suddenly flew out of it and away into the distance. I remembered then, how a long time ago in India another bird had flown out of a glossy hedge of green leaves, uttering the same sharp cry, and I had run towards the spot from which it had taken flight, parted the leaves and seen revealed my first nest filled with fledgelings. Carefully inserting a hand among the birds, I had felt the small bodies pulsate with warm life. That hedge, and those birds vibrating with life under the hot Indian sky, were as much a part of the country as the sari-clad women, the carved temples, and the chatter of monkeys; the spirit of India had seeped through human flesh, leaf, stone and feather, making each plant, building and creature irrevocably hers. I could no more imagine those Indian fledgelings elsewhere than I could a nest of English thrushes set in a hawthorn bush and surrounded by meadows being anywhere but in these islands. For some minutes I was back again in India, and I remembered my promise as the great liner had sailed away from the Far East: one day I'll come back. . .

A strong wind had got up. I walked through the gardens and fields, climbed over the wall, and after some ten minutes I came to the long avenue of copper beeches. I had the feeling as I walked along the avenue of trees that I had briefly slipped out of the current of time. The roar of the wind and tossing of the branches, the grass under my feet, were all that I was aware of. And with every step I took I drew closer to them until the line enclosing my separate existence melted. I was the wind, the grass, the trees, and a human being, nameless and without identity, separated from nothing and no one.

This feeling of non-separation lasted until I opened the door of the trailer and stepped inside. Then I gradually returned to myself and my mind started to revolve once more round my various problems, desires and joys.

I made myself some tea and sat down to do some mending. Hardly had I threaded the needle than I remembered my packet of mail, still unread, lying at the bottom of the wardrobe. I took it out and started to slit open the envelopes. There was a letter from my Arab correspondent, Ahmed; another from an Indian girl, Tara, who lived in a town in South India near the Western Ghats.

Ahmed was a married man and the father of two children, yet like most of my friends, he was extremely mobile and thought nothing of crossing over from Aden to the East African coast to take up a job there for some months. In his letter he wrote of going later that year to cosmopolitan Tangier. He was an ardent nationalist in the Arab movement and wanted to see how things were shaping in other parts of the Islamic world. He suggested that we each travel halfway from our respective countries and meet up at Tangier. We had often discussed, via letters, a meeting in the past, but circumstances had not favoured one as yet.

Tara, unlike most of my other correspondents, had never travelled far from the town in which she had been born. She told me in her letter about a recent festival and various small events connected with her family. 'When are you returning to India?' she asked. 'Do not leave your trip until your next incarnation!'

I took note of addresses and various information my correspondents had given me, then I tore up the letters and pushed the bits into the stove.

Of a sudden, I felt unbearably restless and longed to be off to some eastern country. I walked up and down the trailer, peered out of the windows, scrubbed a few vegetables for supper. Then Jai came in and stood for some moments in the doorway, and it was as though I saw him for the first and the last time, and I burst into tears.

'Whatever's the matter?' he asked.

But I was unable to tell him.

The wind had grown to gale force. Every so often the trailer would rock slightly under its impact. I lit the paraffin lamps and the flames cast a warm light about the room. Betty was curled up in her basket, and Jai and I sat at the table, he whittling flowers and I colouring them. Outside was storm, darkness and hissing rain, while inside there was warmth and light.

I woke up during that night and it seemed that the wind had increased still more in volume. Branches snapped and came hurtling down into the yard and rain hissed against the panes. Whenever the wind abated a little I could hear the big dogs outside turning restlessly in their straw-filled boxes. I laid a hand on Jai's head and sat up in bed. He did not wake.

The stove was still burning low and the temperature in the room felt pleasantly warm. I drew back a curtain and looked at the varying shades of darkness outside. A flurry of leaves was swept against the pane and swept away again. I would never be able to explain to Jai why it was that loving him and having come to him of my own free will, I would be leaving him against the desire of my own heart to travel my own road in a world that would often seem dark and unbearably lonely. We had spent a little time together. Now our time was up and I must be going again.

The next morning after breakfast I started to pack my belongings.

'What are you doing?' he asked.

'I'm leaving you,' I said. 'I love you, but I'm leaving you. Don't ask me why, because I could never explain.'

He smiled. 'I thought I had won,' he said. 'Well, I won't ask any questions or try and persuade you again to stay. Be happy wherever you go, sweetheart. I'll always remember you. Perhaps one day you'll come back to me.'

'Perhaps,' I said, but I knew I never would.

I kissed him, then glanced out of a window. 'There's no one about, so I'll go now. Say goodbye to Fanny and the rest for me.'

I opened the trailer door and stepped out into the bleak, grey morning. Without looking back, I walked quickly across the yard, and when I had reached the far end I heard the door of the wagon close.

SIXTEEN

Find a Way or Make One

DURING the years which followed I did a certain amount of travelling in Britain and overseas. Between these intervals of travel were grim, sedentary periods spent working in offices and living in bedsitters. My trips abroad took me as far as Morocco and Tangier.

Whenever office life became unendurable I would hand in my notice and set off for the countryside. But these periods of release from the monotonous grind of an office existence only made matters worse: I felt more strongly that I could not bear to return to London, to set my feet on the treadmill again. Yet I always did return, and for two reasons. The first was the ease with which I could pick up a job there, even during the winter season. And the second: much as I loathed the life of office, tube, and bedsitter, it was the only way I managed to find a little free time to write. It was through my writing that I intended to gain my release from financial insecurity.

During these city periods I lived and worked mainly among people with whom I had nothing in common. And I came to know the sheer awfulness of lodging in other people's homes in cramped and dingy bedsitters, and I experienced the insecurity of being turned out of some miserable room at a week's notice and having to find, somehow, new lodgings during the brief after-office hours.

After I had returned to London from yet another flight to the country, with a few pounds in my purse to tide me over the days until I found a job, I resolved that this time I would stay until I had completed a book, and got it accepted by a publisher. I simply had to tether myself indefinitely to a highly uncongenial way of life in order to free myself from it.

After lodging in unpleasant company in the Paddington area for a short spell, I was fortunate in finding lodgings with two very nice old ladies in a pleasant part of London. Here I was able to work at last without interruption. The only snag about this room was that the cooking arrangements consisted of a single gas ring. My health and digestion had deteriorated, and I felt that I must have a stove of sorts on which to cook my meals. But I would have done better to stick to this room and risk chronic indigestion. I moved and struck a series of lodgings each one worse than the last. Time was running against me; I knew that I could not stand much more of this life. My weight, which is normally around nine stone, had dropped to just over seven, and my face was a permanent shade of putty. With each passing day I found it more difficult to concentrate on my work in the evenings, and I wasted long hours sitting listlessly by the gas fire doing nothing more strenuous than gazing into space.

Once, long ago – or so it seemed now – I lived alone on a hilltop and been perfectly happy in my solitude. Life had taken on new depth and width. Now, living by myself in a bedsitter and making my way through the London crowds, loneliness would often sweep over me. And loneliness, I discovered, narrows life. It can be a prison. I asked myself again: how I was to free myself, experience the opening up of life once more?

Eventually my first book came out. Although it was well received the pleasure I gained on that score was cancelled out by the behaviour of the press, who made my life every kind of hell. So much so that I decided to leave the country. Journalists – reporters and writers of gossip columns – pitter-pattered busily between my last office, my bank, and my last lodgings interrogating all and sundry in the hope of gaining information about me and my whereabouts. Maps were printed in some newspapers of the areas in which the pressmen thought I was most likely to be, and human bloodhounds did everything they could to track me down. Letters, which various acquaintances had addressed to my lodging, were handed over to the press, were opened, and the senders interviewed in the hope they might supply further gossip about me. And various persons, some of whom I had only met once or twice in my life, racked their brains for any tiny bit of information they thought might be of interest to the newshounds. I was thankful then that all my private mail was still being sent care of the Stratford Post Office throughout my stay in London, in spite of the inconvenience this sometimes caused me.

The columns of several dailies were flashing such headlines as: 'Landlady says. . .' 'Always dresses in tweeds and flat-heeled shoes. . .' 'Terrified of success. . .' 'Has made huge fortune. . .'

As regards the huge fortune, while the book brought me a modest financial gain, it was nothing like the fantastic sums given out in the press, after Inland Revenue had taken their bite.

Life in Britain had become quite impossible for me after the publication of *Seal Morning*. I gave up the long-cherished hope that with money earned from the book I might at long last be able to buy a small croft in Western Scotland or a cottage in the Evesham area. I had been looking forward to this possibility more than anything else; of being able to buy myself a home, of having my own roof over my head, a place where I could work till three o'clock in the morning if I felt like it, or fling a frying pan of eggs and chips across the kitchen without having a landlady peering round the door and saying – 'You can take a week's notice!' Only someone who has done a stretch in digs can know the yearning, which at times approaches almost an obsession, to have a place of one's own, be it only a one-roomed shack. But this hope of mine was destined to remain in the realm of dreams.

I left Britain to become a wanderer once more, homeless, of no fixed address, I cut myself off.

My spirits were so low on leaving England that I can recall hardly anything about the voyage.

I visited Tangier for the second time. It is not a place where I would want to live for long, but it is very pleasant for a short stay. I lay on the beach and slept – I felt I could have slept for weeks on end. The Berber women, wearing wide straw hats, came in from the Rif mountains on their little donkeys with goods to sell at the market. A score of nationalities thronged the crowded streets. Gradually my spirits revived and my weight returned to normal. I sat in the open-air cafés and went for excursions into the hilly countryside. Then I moved on to the Far East and India.

I visited remote Indian villages and ancient temples with wide steps leading down to bathing tanks covered with lotus blossoms. Sometimes out in the country along lonely roads I met parties of Gypsies with their bullock carts and animals. The women were dressed in worn red saris, their arms and ankles laden with bangles. The men had long, unkempt hair, sometimes done up in a bun, and a wild, direct gaze. They would swarm about me, demanding baksheesh with outstretched hands, or try to sell me a trifle for a price twenty times beyond its value. Often, as the noisy crowd of vagabonds disappeared down the road, the landscape about me – the palms and the hot, red earth – would seem to fade from sight and be replaced in my mind's eye by distant scenes and faces. I would see a log fire burning in the dusk, and close by it wagons and trailers. The faces of men, women, and children I once knew would reappear again, and one face in particular would return at these moments to haunt me. I would hear his voice say, 'I thought I had won. . .' But if neither of us had won, I realised now, in this ancient land from which his remote ancestors had once set out on their long journey to Europe, that neither of us had lost either.

Sometimes I wonder whether it will be long until the last British Gypsy stands upon the hill to gaze on the countryside, before disappearing into the shadows of the past, like the wandering minstrels of long ago. If so, his sojourn on this planet must be counted a unique and colourful one and his departure a matter for regret. The Gypsy lives out for all of us, whatever our nationality or occupation, that which we truly are, travellers of vast and windswept regions whose myriad journeyings will only cease with the ending of time.